SECURITY FOR SENIOR CITIZENS

How To Make
The Golden Years Safer Years

by
DAVID Y. COVERSTON
Illustrated by
ANNE C. BROWN

SECURITY SEMINARS PRESS
Ocala, Florida

Library of Congress Catologing-in-Publication Data
Coverston, David Y. (David Yost), 1920-
   Security for senior citizens.
   Includes index.
      1. Aged--United States--Crime against--Prevention.
      2. Crime prevention--United States--Citizen participation.
      3. Dwellings--United States--Security measures. I. Title.
   HV6250.4.A34C686 1988 362.8'8 87-12885

ISBN   0-936101-03-2
         0-936101-02-4 (pbk.)

Cover Design By: Cover Typography By:
  Wendy J. Ward   Tammy R. Garst

Published in the United States of America
Book Design and Typography by **FAST TYPE, Inc.**

Published by Security Seminars Press (Publishers)
3400 S.E. 35th Street
P.O. Box 70162
Ocala, Florida 32670
904- 694 6185

ACKNOWLEDGEMENTS

The author wishes to thank the Senior Citizens interviewed during the writing of this book. Their insight and experiences in dealing with life provided much background material.

Individuals contributing to these pages were numerous, but special thanks go to the following named individuals.

To Stephanie Matthews for her word processing skills and suggestions.

To Maury and Sandy Swee, typographers and computer consultants, for their words of wisdom and guidance.

To my daughter, Anne C. Brown, Illustrator and candid critic, for her line drawings and love.

To my daughter Lucinda J. Coverston, for her assistance in keeping the production orderly and for her affection.

To my brother Sam, for his suggestions, critique of copy, and pushing me to write and meet deadlines.

And, to my wife, Martha, for her encouragement, wisdom, patience, and caring.

DEDICATION

Our nation is growing older - our population is aging. The proportion of citizens over fifty in the general population increases each day.

This is causing major changes in many facets of our society. Mandatory retirement requirements regarding age have been abolished in most sectors of private and public life. Discrimination due to age is illegal. Those of us in our "golden years" are recognized as citizens who have earned their spurs and are capable of using them.

However - one great need in our society must be resolved, and quickly - the need of senior citizens for protection and physical security. The increase in crime at all levels, the overloading of law enforcement agencies, and the failure of the private sector to become more involved in protecting themselves and others are reasons for this great need.

As time has marched - and we have marched with it - our reflexes have slowed. Our eyes seek larger print. Our ears ask for louder and slower words. Our voices command closer attention. Our touch is not as sensitive, and our nose sometimes plays tricks on us.

We realize our general awareness is less sharp. Events that grab the attention of energy rich juniors fail to impress us. We ignore much we once considered important.

The criminal element in society takes note of our diminishing physical ability. They know it is more difficult for us to protect our persons, properties, and other possessions. They prefer us as victims.

To older and less agile citizens, this book is dedicated. May it help make "the golden years" safer years.

CONTENTS

SECURITY FOR SENIOR CITIZENS

PREFACE

During the time a name for this book was being considered, numbers of suggestions were offered. They ranged from "Guarding Gray Hairs" to "Babysitting Second Childhooders". Some were silly; some were funny, and some just didn't fit.

The author, however, is a member of this group and wanted a dignified yet descriptive title. He found the word "senior" denotes those over others in rank or length of service. He found "citizens" are those in whom are entrusted certain duties, rights, and privileges. Thus - a Senior Citizen is one over others in length of service and is a person in whom one places trust.

The use of the pronouns "we", "our", and "us" throughout the text is intentional. Writing for my peer group, I will be a part of the scenario.

If any information gained from this work helps to prevent a crime; saves anyone from the pain, humiliation, and loss of a personal attack; and/or protects property or other possessions from criminal acts or vandalism, it will be worth the effort it has taken to write it.

As seniors, we have seen and accomplished a great deal. As citizens, it is our duty to help make this world a safer place in which to live - for ourselves and for others. If we work at it, we can, indeed, make our "GOLDEN YEARS OUR SAFER YEARS".

Chapter 1

As Time Goes By

TRANSITION

As we move from middle age to senior citizen status, we are reminded by the line from a Willie Nelson song, "Funny, How Time Slips Away". (Copyright 1986 EMI of America Records, A Division of Capitol Records, Incorporated)

Subtle changes take place in our way of life; our pace slows. Our eyes are less apt to detect danger. Ears fail to pick up warnings. Touch is less sensitive, and the nostrils lose some of their ability to differentiate. Food tastes different. We are enduring the aging process - and we face special security problems.

A common security problem, one we share with the general population, is the continuing rise in the crime rate.

Murder, rape, assault with a deadly weapon, vandalism, fraud, burglary, robbery, and auto theft occur all to frequently. The cost in pain, humiliation, and loss of valuables is horrendous.

Senior Citizens are not cringing and fear ridden individuals. Fear of crime is not their greatest fear. News stories tell how many ladies and gentlemen aged sixty and over successfully fight off attackers and others of the criminal element. Senior Citizens are brave and courageous citizens - citizens most likely to become involved in situations where help is needed.

SPECIAL PROBLEMS

Senior Citizens do have special problems when faced with the problems of protection and physical security. The criminal, including those with criminal intent, seeks Seniors as potential victims. They think all Seniors are feeble and decrepit.

The truth is Senior Citizens are inclined to think the world is safer than it is. They tend to be trusting with empathy for others. These traits which endear them to the world also make them vulnerable to crime and other hazards. Let us review some of the special security problems Seniors should remember.

CRIMINALS

Senior Citizens have no reason to analyze the criminal mind, but they need to know how it works. The criminal mind may not be a smart mind, but it is almost always a shrewd mind. The criminal mind is ever seeking the easiest way to take advantage of others. Criminals, for the most part, are basically cowards - dangerous cowards. They look for odds in their favor. They like dark areas of the world and lone subjects. They like unlocked doors, open windows, and empty hallways. Criminals have warped minds and distorted value systems. Criminals do not like to attack confident appearing and confident acting individuals because criminals are basically cowards - dangerous cowards.

Those of us reaching the age of sixty in the United States have reached the age group possessing over 60% of the national wealth. We are past the peak of physical strength. Criminals are aware of this. Purse snatchers, pickpockets, robbers, burglars, rapists (no female is immune to this crime), and con men prefer to attack the elderly - particularly the solvent appearing.

Senior Citizens can win the ongoing battle against crime and criminals. They can do so by taking the odds away from the criminal element and creating odds in their favor. It may require a severe adjustment in life style, and it will require strict attention to danger signals.

The first step is to become security minded. It is mandatory if we are to survive. And, unless it becomes habitual, there can be no freedom from the fear of bodily harm - no peace of mind regarding the safety of material possessions.

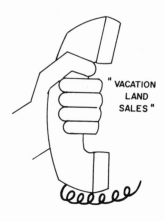

CON ARTISTS

Con men and women are criminals in a number of disguises. They dress as investment counselors, aluminum siding salespersons, driveway repair experts, roofers, peddlers, charity organization collectors, legal advisors, magazine subscription takers, and other types of entrepreneurs. They come in person - they use the mail system - and they love to use the telephone - especially at dinner time!

The Senior Citizen is a favorite of the boiler room pitch artist and the pigeon drop specialist. These scummy characters are, for the most part, charming and glib. It is difficult to cull legitimate offers from the bogus at times, but it can be done. It requires close attention, common sense, and courage. By refusing to be hurried into making a decision, by making discreet inquiries, and by having the courage to report suspected flim- flam deals, you are in command. Remember, if it sounds to good to be true - it probably is! Anyone with a legitimate offer will give you as much time as you wish in order to make your decision and will be glad to have you confirm they have a bona fide proposition.

LOCATION

The geographical location of residence causes security problems for many Senior Citizens. Many have moved to cities and/or states they are not familiar with, or in some cases, to another area in their same community.

The new residential area may have different ordinances and laws. The living conditions in the new neighborhood may be drastically different. Moving from a large home with plenty of room in Ohio to a small mobile home in Florida or Arizona can be a traumatic experience.

Migration figures indicate many Senior Citizens move from cities where the crime rate is high to other cities in the belief they will be safer in a new locale. The move may be made within the same state. However - the same figures give evidence the new city may have as much, or perhaps more, crime than the old city. Before making a permanent move, Seniors should carefully check out many details about their proposed new home. Visit the area; talk with residents, and ask the local law enforcement personnel where the safest side of town is located.

Moving to a warm climate in the sunbelt may not solve security problems because the criminal element likes warmer weather too!!! Another factor to be considered in re-locating is the density of the population in the new area. Senior Citizens tend to congregate in clusters and high density brings special security needs.

RESIDENTIAL AND MOBILE HOME SUBDIVISIONS

Retirement subdivisions are usually areas consisting of single family dwellings, including townhouses, or multi-family units. Most such subdivisions have a much higher percentage of Senior Citizens than the normal cross section of society. This means the inhabitants are in the age group least likely to commit a crime but are also in the age group most vulnerable to criminal acts.

Before moving into any retirement subdivision, major items need to be thoroughly investigated. It is important to note the number of entrance and exit roads of the subdivision and their physical condition. This is especially true in areas subject to hurricanes, floods, and/or earthquakes. Entrance and exit roads are important factors in planning for fire, police, and security protection as well as for deployment of all types of emergency vehicles.

In evaluating retirement subdivisions, close attention should be paid to the kind of, if any, perimeter barriers that exist. Walls, fences, and other impediments to auto and/or foot traffic tend to discourage criminals.

In making security surveys of retirement subdivisions, it will be wise to note the condition of the streets, the location of utility lines, and rules as to the parking of extra vehicles, boats, and campers. The maximum height to which shrubbery is allowed to grow, and any restrictions on fences, should be taken into consideration. The greater the clutter and the less open space present, the better the chances are for the criminally intent to move about with little chance of being recognized.

The mobile home or manufactured home community should receive even closer scrutiny when being checked for security factors. Ordinarily they are placed much closer together in a subdivision. By their nature, they are more easily broken into and are subject to greater damage.

The first consideration, from a security standpoint, is to determine whether the mobile home community is composed of individually owned lots, or whether the lots are commonly owned by others. If the lots are commonly owned and controlled, check the type of security in place. If the lots are individually owned, security is the responsibility of the individual homeowner.

In individually owned lot areas, the same survey used for residential subdivision investigation may be followed. In a community of mobile homes where lots are owned by other than the dwellers, the amenities offered need to be studied. The kind of security force is on duty and what are visitor regulations are questions that need to be addressed.

Mobile and manufactured homes are not as sturdy as stick built homes and security requirements for those who live in them are greater. The need for upgrading windows and doors, the installation of fire and burglar alarms, and the locking requirements are more pronounced than for conventionally constructed houses.

TRANSPORTATION

The lack of public transportation facilities in many areas poses security problems for many Senior Citizens. Driving skills fade as our sight, hearing, and muscular reflexes diminish. Then, there is the fact many Seniors have never learned to drive. Women, in particular, may have a long history of having had someone else doing the driving and, thus, never learned the skill. When the person or persons who drove are no longer available, the senior may find out how it feels to sit behind the steering wheel. Learning to drive at an advanced age

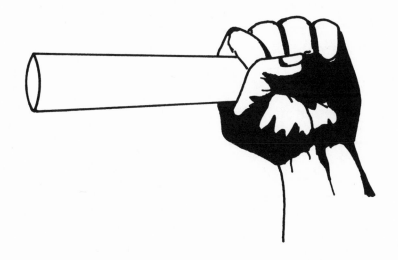

is difficult, and the driver may never become a really safe driver. However - we are never to old to learn. If we are physically able and properly taught, most of us can learn to drive safely. It is often a must be learned skill, and everyone feels more comfortable in emergency situations when they know how to drive.

Trips by methods other than automobile require other security precautions. Bus stations and railroad depots are not always located in crime free locations. Consult with ticket agents for bus terminals and railroad stations as to security measures in place. Airline security is becoming more stringent with terrorist activities in mind, but we must not let our guards down. Keep your eyes peeled for anyone who seems suspicious on the ground, in the terminal, and among boarding passengers.

When going aboard a seagoing ship, check for fire extinguishers, lifeboats, life jackets, escape hatches, compartment doors, and gangways.

THE AUTOMOBILE

The automobile is the favorite and most often used form of transportation in the U.S. Be sure the one you drive has a decent spare tire, an easy to use and sturdy jack, a toolbox, and emergency road gear. Proper maintenance performed on a regular basis, additional physical equipment, plus using caution in parking will alleviate many auto security problems. And, as always - use common sense.

A number of motor clubs and the American Association of Retired Persons are reliable sources of information regarding safe operation of automobiles. Remember - driving an auto is the most dangerous thing most of us will ever do, and it becomes more dangerous each day.

TRAVEL

Traveling the highways, skyways, and byways of the world is a major activity of Senior Citizens. Travelers are subjected to a greater variety of situations requiring tight security measures than any other civilian group. On the go - for business or pleasure - the frame of mind tends to lead to careless moments. We forget, during our adventures, and do not take proper precautions. It is true, none of us are completely safe anywhere or at anytime in the world, but extra vigilance while on the road is a must.

Strange faces and strange places along with strange languages and strange surroundings are on our travel agenda. The security list needs to be double checked.

When checking in for a night's lodging - anywhere - the first question asked should be, what type of security is afforded? This is to be followed by a query as to how to contact security and the response time that may be expected.

A motel or hotel employee should show you to your room. A search of the room to make sure no one is hiding therein and a check of all electrical and water facilities should be conducted. Windows and doors should be checked for signs of previous forced entry. Note should be taken of the location of the room as to accessibility by intruders. The location of exit doors and fire extinguishers is a security must.

If you are not comfortable with your room assignment, ask to be moved. Those catering to the public pay huge liability insurance fees and are anxious to avoid situations which will bring a horde of greedy lawyers attempting to get settlements from insurance carriers for any reason.

A small investment in a room smoke detector and door guard will help your peace of mind and perhaps save your life. Many portable models are on the market, and they take little space in a suitcase.

Use the safekeeping facilities of your lodging host to store your valuables. Jewelry, watches, cameras, and cash are favorite targets of the hotel and motel thief. Do not tempt them.

MOVING

If you are moving across town, to another city, to another state, or to another country - take time to plan a safe and secure move. Moving companies are ordinarily reliable, but don't take chances. Investigate your mover before you make a commitment. Find out the kind of insurance they carry, the kind of guarantees they give, and their overall reputation.

After you have chosen your mover, make arrangements well in advance of your planned moving day. Plan times of departure, estimated stopovers, and time of arrival. Plot your movers route and make sure several reliable people with your interests at heart have copies. The same information on you and your family should be with the same people.

If you cannot be present when the movers come to pick up your possessions, have your representative there. The mover should show identification and give you the names of all employees being used. The make, color, and license plate of the mover's vehicle or vehicles should be written alongside the other information obtained and the exact time of departure noted. Most movers will give the route they plan to take.

You or your representative must be at your new residence when the mover is ready to unload.

An inspection of goods is required in the event of damaged or missing articles in order to file an insurance claim. Do not give your mover the keys to your old or new residence.

If you move on your own, precautions to take will be outlined in a later chapter which will have more details on moving.

NEIGHBORS

A great force for security in any neighborhood, maligned though they may be, is the nosy neighbor. Your neighbors know the kind of car you drive. They know the number of persons in your household. They know the time of day you leave home, and they know what time you return. They know a great deal about you and your habits - just as you know about them.

Nosy neighbors may be a pain in the neck at times, but they can make your existence a safer one. They can spot a strange car in your driveway - identify callers at your home - and take care of mail and package deliveries during your absence.

When you leave on any extended trip, let your neighbors know where you are going, how you can be reached in an emergency, and when you are going to return. Nosy neighbors have been known to rout vandals, report burglaries and fires, and do other things for the neighborhood. All it takes is the time to leave addresses and telephone numbers.

WORK

Many Seniors continue working long past retirement age. They plan to stay employed as long as they are physically and mentally able. Workplaces vary in the degree of security they afford. We working Seniors must be more attuned to security measures than younger workers because, like it or not, we have diminished response capabilities.

Inside work requires more than passing knowledge of fire potential. Rules and regulations to be followed and actions to be taken in the event of fire should be committed to memory. Seniors should join other workers and insist regular fire drills be held. Every worker, and especially Seniors, should know, to the second, how long it takes to get from any work station to which they may be assigned to the outside of the building via any and all evacuation routes. They should know the location of, and learn how to operate, all fire extinguishers in their work areas.

Inside workers need to know the security plans for such natural disasters as hurricanes, tornadoes, and earthquakes. Senior workers must know the rules their employer has established in the event of a robbery. If no rules are present, they should be instigated. Many employees are hurt or killed in robbery situations because they either panic or decide to interfere with the robbers.

Senior workers need to know where first aid supplies are kept and how to use them. They are usually calm in first aid situations and are excellent employees to be made responsible for the replenishment of first aid supplies.

A list of emergency numbers to be called with actions to be taken in any kind of emergency should be at every work station. Outside workers need to know the security measures that apply to inside workers plus a few additional. Senior Citizens working outside need to take greater care in the operation of outdoor equipment and tools than younger colleagues due to slower reflexes. Seniors should also pay close attention to overexposure to cold or heat since they are more susceptible to heat exhaustion and hypothermia.

All outside employees should memorize the actions to be taken in the event of any kind of disturbance - whether caused by human or natural forces.

PLAY

Senior Citizens take part in many and varied recreational activities. Golf courses, bowling alleys, boating marinas, fishing camps, hunting areas, tennis courts, and firing ranges teem with Seniors. They frequent shuffle board courts, bingo parlors, fishing piers, dance halls, and gambling casinos. A security problem exists in each and every place.

We need protection while we play. We must alert ourselves to the dangers present at or on our playing area and be prepared to cope with them. Locker rooms provide hiding places for thieves, robbers, and rapists. Wallets, purses, and sporting goods are favorite prey of criminals haunting recreational areas. As a customer of any facility, you should insist on the establishment of sound security measures.

Camping is a form of recreation that has become more communal than the lone wilderness camping the word usually brings to mind. Commercial campgrounds and facilities at state and federal parks furnish amenities that have taken the edge off of "roughing it". However - take care when entering any camping area. A thorough check of the location is a must. Know where restrooms and showers are in relation to your campsite and note the lighting along the routes to and from it. Check these routes out before dark and make sure you know where to go and whom to call in case of an emergency. Map out evacuation trails and make sure all in your party are aware of them. Do not let the fascination of an open fire cause you to lose sight of safety measures and remember to keep fires confined to authorized places. A few minutes working out a security plan for your camping adventure may save your life.

Bowling alleys attract pickpockets, locker looters, purse snatchers, and robbers. Parking lots around alleys offer muggers and rapists golden opportunities. Vandals and auto thieves find bowling alley parking areas a fertile territory in which to operate. The criminal knows bowlers tend to leave lanes at late hours, tired, mind occupied, and perhaps ultra-relaxed from a good night libation. They view senior bowlers as easy targets, but by keeping our guards up and our wits about us - they can be fooled. Carrying your keys at ready, perhaps on a "Nasprotector Key Keeper", having a flashlight, and using care in approaching your vehicle are musts in the bowling alley parking lot.

Practically every playing area is attractive to the criminal. They operate on the theory participants are in a state of relaxation and are more vulnerable when in a recreational atmosphere. It gives the shrewd lawbreaker an opportunity to disguise themselves in playing gear to gain access to locker rooms, parking areas, and clubhouses. If your primary recreation sites are without guarded entrances and other types of security - talk to management about the situation.

Another playing field security problem faced by Seniors is that of proper medication while being a participant. Before starting any match, if you are on medication, inform your partners of dosages, times, and other pertinent information. No medicine works if used improperly.

A list of any allergies should be on your person. Many people have died from insect stings triggered by an already present allergy. Med Alert bracelets are important at the recreational site, and you are doing your partners and opponents a favor if you have advised them of any medical problems. They want to best you in the contest - not take you to the hospital.

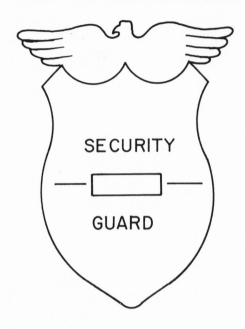

LAW ENFORCEMENT

Senior Citizens have excellent opportunities to become acquainted with law enforcement personnel. The county sheriff, the chief of police, and their staff are keenly aware of the problems in our society. Overworked, underpaid, and seldom praised, our lawpersons go that extra mile. We should make it a point to get to know as many law officers as we can. They are interested in good auxiliary men and women - find out the requirements and spread the word. Join your neighborhood watch programs and attend "Help Stop Crime" programs. Learn about the sheriff's posse and how you might participate. As the friendly "McGruff" advises - "Help Take a Bite Out of Crime".

SECURITY PERSONNEL

Security forces are different from law enforcement forces. Their job is to prevent crime by guarding persons and premises. The mere fact they are on duty is a great deterrent to criminal activity. They are, for the most part, underpaid, bear great responsibility, have little or no official authority, and are generally unknown. If Sir Winston Churchill had described them he might have said, "No force does so much for so many with so little as does the security personnel force."

The image of physical security personnel has been improving rapidly, and one of the reasons has been the influx of Senior Citizens into the working field of physical security. Their experience, their ability to handle people, and their "common sense" makes them greatly desired employees in a profession that is truly in need of employees with "people knowledge".

SPECIFICS

In the chapters to follow, you will find many specific recommendations - recommendations to be strongly considered as you take steps to make your "golden years safer years".

As you read them - adopt those you feel are appropriate for your use. Add to the lists for your personal physical security program. The burden of providing your personal physical security is - as have been most things during your life - on your shoulders.

Titles of chapters will address major subjects to be covered in the chapter. However - it will be evident that physical security measures cross and re-cross one another in many instances. This results in some duplication - but any measure of protection worth using is also worth repeating.

Chapters are devoted to the automobile, the workplace, the home, the recreational field, the streets, sidewalks, and stores. Other chapters will address travel, first aid, and fire. A final chapter ties it all together and is entitled "ET CETERA".

This book was written specifically for Senior Citizens, but it contains material and information needed by all citizens. As one senior put it at the end of an interview, "Everyone gets old if they live long enough, and this may help them live long enough". The author enjoyed the many interviews with fellow Senior Citizens. He learned a great deal in researching the subject. If one person benefits from the contents contained herein, it will have been worth the time and effort it took to write it.

KEEP ME LIT!

Chapter 2
HOME SWEET HOME

Our homes are our castles, and we must build moats around them. The moats we create will be different from the water and dragon filled canals that surrounded feudal castles. Ours will consist of fences, alarm systems, doors with dead bolts, firmly fastened windows, barking dogs, and nosy neighbors to name a few.

Whatever type of residence we have chosen, it must be made as secure as possible. Our lives and our possessions need all the protection we can give them from dangerous humans, fire, and fickle nature.

Single family dwellings have different security requirements than multiple family unit dwellings, and the requirements for either do not fit the mobile or manufactured home.

THE PHYSICAL SECURITY SURVEY

By making a physical survey of the residence, we can find many specific things that need to be done to make our home a safer place in which to live. Some may need only minor corrections, some may need major corrections, and we may find a need for some new installations.

As we prepare to make our physical survey, let us remember burglary is the number one crime in America, and - burglars look for pushovers. Statistics from interviews with convicted burglars reveal the burglar wants and needs to obtain entrance to a house within four minutes of the approach. If they are unable to make entry into a house within four minutes, they ordinarily seek an easier house to burglarize.

Burglars and other criminals are basically cowards. They look for the unlocked door or the unlatched window. They hide in overgrown shrubbery, using it to cover their activities. They like houses without yard lights, and they despise a house with a barking dog in the yard.

Movie stereotypes of burglars with picks that enable them to open any door fit few modern day thieves. Most tools used to get into houses are ordinary tools found in and around most homes. Garden tools, screwdrivers, hammers, pliers, and prying tools are favorites. Most of these are picked up around the house that is the object of burglary!

Before we begin our physical security survey - make a mental note of the first rule in home protection - *"Don't be careless; don't make it easy for the intruder"*.

THE EXTERIOR PHYSICAL SURVEY

A camera is an indispensable tool to use in making any physical security survey. The kind of camera or film is not important. The important thing is to hold the camera steady and make clear and revealing pictures. A polaroid, 35mm, or even an old box camera will do the job. The pictures will help your insurance agent compile a rate for homeowners coverage. The pictures will also allow you to make an analysis of potential security problems and to perfect a plan to correct any existing.

Load your camera, walk into the street in front of your house, and take a picture of the front. Move to a position where you can see not only the front but also one side of your house and take another picture. Repeat the process so that you have a picture of the other side of the house. If your house has areas hidden from your camera on these three shots, such as a closed courtyard, move in to those areas and picture them in full detail. The same goes for any alcoves or other styles of architecture that keep your camera's inquiring eye from getting details.

While taking pictures, note possible hiding places a person might use in your landscape plantings. Note areas that should be lighted at night to afford the greatest visibility. A mental note made at the time the pictures are taken will come back and help you make a better analysis when the photos are developed.

After you have taken the pictures, make a close study of approaches to the house. Note the condition of walkways and driveways. Cracks in concrete or oil collected on the surface may cause a person to trip and fall. Remember - accidents do not happen - they are caused. Security not only includes protecting ourselves from others but also from ourselves. If animals, domestic or otherwise, have dug holes in the soil, fill them and tamp them. Pay attention to overhanging limbs and shrubbery growing that hides the view from windows and/or doors. Those determined to be a detriment to safety should be pruned immediately. Gates and fences, if any, should be in good condition.

Before leaving the front of the house, inspect the front door. If it is not a solid wood or metal door, plan to replace it. Once a solid wood or metal door is in place, it should have a "peep hole" or wide angle lens installed so the entrance can be seen from inside without the door being opened. If it does not have a deadbolt - install one.

Look at all windows to determine if previous forced entry signs are present. Test the windows and window frames. Broken panes and/or locks need replacement at once.

If the garage or carport opens to the front - check it carefully. Open garages and garages with doors unlocked are an invitation to burglars and vandals. Never leave a garage door open or unlocked unless you are present. Criminals use garages as places in which to hide, then as a base for further mischief after you have left the house or have gone inside. The garage door must have a locking system difficult to breach.

Carports are ideal places to temporarily store many items the vandal or burglar likes to have available. Step ladders, hand tools, gardening tools, and other implements left in the open may be used as entry tools. Their favorites are hammers, screwdrivers, pliers, and any tool with a cutting edge to be used as a prying instrument.

Now- take your camera to the back of the house. Take a shot from directly in back and one from each corner showing the rear and the side. If indentations or courtyards, etc. obstruct, shoot until you have all outside exteriors.

As you did in front, observe condition of patios, lanai's, outbuildings, walkways, and driveways. Check the condition of tree limbs and shrubbery and remove those compromising security. Many homeowners use varieties of cactus and other thorny plants under rear windows to discourage peeping toms, burglars, and vandals.

After the exterior has been pictured and inspected - try this: make believe you want to enter the house but do not have a key. Your search around the house for a so-called "hidden key" should convince you that hiding a key is foolish. Burglars are experts in finding "hidden keys" and insurance payments are hard to come by if no evidence of breaking and entering is found. It is preferable to leave a key with a trusted neighbor (in the event you lose your keys) who might also need them in case of an emergency.

While practicing your attempt to enter the house without a key, use anything you have on your person. Credit cards, other keys, fingernail files, combs, bobby pins, letter openers, and the like can be used to pry open windows and even doors locks. A garden hoe or rake handle makes a good lever to use in prying open sliding glass doors. A length of wood in the door track will stop this kind of entry.

The point in doing the exercise you have just completed is to convince you that if you can get into your house without a key - what is to prevent a burglar or vandal from doing the same? Take away the easy opportunity.

Another observation you can make while on "the enter without a key" mission is where to locate exterior floodlights. Criminals and vandals detest lights. Floodlights deter criminal and vandal actions and can be used to highlight the exterior of the house. Photoelectric cells may be used to turn the lights on at dark and off at daybreak. Ideally, all walls of the house will be lighted, with special emphasis on doorways and garage entrances.

DOORS

Exterior doors should be, at a minimum, one and a quarter inches thick. They should be of solid construction - wood or metal. A wide angle lens (peep hole) should be at occupants eye level in the center of the door. If a great difference in height of occupants exists within a household, two wide angled should be installed. Doors should have non-removable hinges if hinges are exposed. All exterior doors should have dead bolt locks.

Interior doors do not have to be as sturdy as exterior doors, except those sealing the house proper from a vulnerable area such as the garage.

Sliding glass doors require special treatment since they are one of the favorite entry points of intruders. They are also one of the most neglected entry/exit points of the house. Other than remembering to keep them secure, the most important thing is to see they have the proper hardware for security. In addition to the simple locking mechanism built into them, several devices are on the market. One is a plastic device to be anchored in the top runner that will flip down against the side of the sliding portion, making entry more difficult. Another is a pin to fit into a hole drilled through one frame of the door and into the other frame. The author prefers to cut an old broom stick or other sturdy piece of wood into the exact length of the exposed bottom track and drop it into the track when the door is closed. It not only stops a pry - it is visible and often prevents any attempt to enter the door.

WINDOWS

The type of window in the house determines the procedures needed to secure them. Jalousy windows, including the centers of jalousy doors, are easy to open. They can be secured by using epoxy glue to glue them into their tracks, then installing interior grilles. If grilles are used, care must be taken that a portion of them are made with breakaway bars to permit exit in emergencies.

Awning, siding, or single hung windows can be secured by drilling holes into the window frame slanting the holes downward. Then, a nail or special metal pin can be inserted into the hole. The pin will resist efforts to open the window. Thieves do not like to break glass because of the noise and the danger of broken glass. These precautions by the homeowner are intended to discourage entry and cause the would be intruder to leave the premises. A determined intruder will get entry into almost any house given time and opportunity.

MULTIPLE UNIT RESIDENCES

Even if you live in a multiple unit residence such as a condominium, townhouse, or apartment complex - you should make a physical security survey. Since you will be sharing much common area with others, it will help if you can get others to join you in a mutual "watchful eye" survey. Expressing your concern for overall security to others, including managers and members of associations, may aid you in making all golden years safer years.

Commonly owned areas are primarily outside areas. Many multiple residential complexes employ in-house security personnel to control entrances and patrol grounds. However - the amenities of many complexes, swimming pools, tennis courts, golf courses, playgrounds, jogging and bicycling lanes, and picnic facilities make it difficult to patrol all areas. Criminals sometimes use these amenities as entry points.

If you live in a multi-family complex, insist uniformed security personnel be employed - around the clock. Well-trained, professionally dressed security personnel in highly visible areas offer one of the most effective deterrents to criminal actions. Most complex owners will be happy to cooperate since it lowers their insurance rates and helps protect them from third party responsibility lawsuits.

MANUFACTURED - MOBILE HOMES

The manufactured or mobile home dweller has another set of security problems. The majority of these units, when first built, are relatively simple to

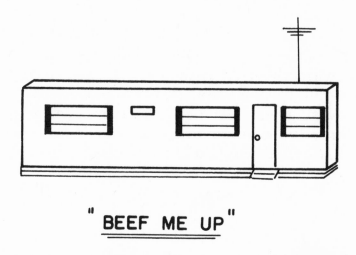

" BEEF ME UP "

break into. Designed for easy maintenance and carefree living, they are vulnerable to burglars and vandals. All owners should take steps to "beef up" these homes.

Every security expert interviewed on the subject of manufactured and mobile homes made recommendations for improving them security wise. They advised adding doors at least one and a quarter inches thick with a deadbolt locking mechanism added. They recommend door frames be either two inch thick wood or hollow steel frames filled with concrete grout. The added strength helps prevent springing doors open with a wedging type tool inserted between door and frame. After the "beef up", adding a wide angle "peep hole" lens is recommended.

Both an advantage and a disadvantage, security wise, manufactured and mobile homes are usually clustered together in parks or subdivisions.

Advantages include closer neighbors, closer attention paid to strangers, and more eyes to report suspicious activities. Disadvantages come from the rapid change in park or subdivision occupancy, long vacations taken by owners, and the fact criminals know Senior Citizens having considerable wealth live in these units.

GARAGES

Garages have been mentioned, but they are so vulnerable and used by so many intruders as a starting point for their activities, they need special attention.

First - make it a habit to always keep the garage locked unless you are present. Second - make sure the locking system is extra tough. The automatic garage door opener has good locking quality. A manually operated garage door ordinarily has a simple lock which is easily compromised. By drilling a hole in the track the door rolls on and inserting a case hardened padlock, its integrity is increased. The case hardened padlock should have both ends engaging the shackle with a minimum of 9/32" shackle and a five pin tumbler.

Garages with swinging doors are not common in new construction, but if you have one, make sure the hasp screw holes or bolts are not visible from the outside.

To repeat - if a door affords entrance to the house from the garage - make it as sturdy as an outside entrance door and equip it with a deadbolt.

EXTERIOR PHYSICAL SURVEY CHECKLIST

Alert Senior Citizens may find or know of additional items to be covered in the security survey. Add them to the list and take steps to remedy any deficiencies. The following list is intended to serve as a reminder of major security problems that need to be addressed, with suggestions for action.

1. Take pictures of front, sides, and rear of house.
2. Mark shrubbery for pruning to eliminate security hazards.
3. Check fences and gates for maintenance problems and locks.
4. Inspect driveways, sidewalks, steps, and stairways for damages.
5. Do away with so called "hidden keys".
6. Store tools and ladders inside.
7. Check doors and windows for signs of unauthorized entry.
8. I install entry doors of solid material with viewing lens and deadbolt.
9. Check to be sure exterior door hinges are non-removable.
10. Secure sliding glass doors with pins and have track blocking insert.
11. Glue panes of jalousy windows and doors and install bars.

12. If windows and/or doors have bars, make some breakaways.

13. Determine positions and install floodlights.

14. Discuss multiple unit residential security with owners/managers.

15. Talk with multiple unit neighbors about security measures.

16. Insist on having uniformed security personnel in complexes.

17. Install pins in windows to prevent easy entry.

18. Upgrade manufactured-mobile home door frames and doors.

19. Check garage doors for adequate locks and keep them locked.

20. Check to see if you can enter your house without a key and without breaking glass or breaking in an entrance door.

THE INTERIOR PHYSICAL SURVEY

Clean off your shoes and enter the front door. Stop. Begin your survey of the interior of your house.

Check the front door - it should be of solid construction, wood or metal. It should contain a wide angle (peep hole) lens. Look through the lens - you should have a full view of the entrance. If you do not have a full view of the entrance, adjust the lens to a full view. The front door should be at least 1-1/4 inches thick with a deadbolt locking mechanism. If a chain latch is attached to the door and the frame facing, consider having it removed. Chain latches tend to give a false sense of security. Anyone with strength can force a door open even if it has a chain latch.

Unlimber your camera before moving into the living room or whatever room is just off the entrance. Take enough pictures to show everything in the room. Antique furniture, grandfather clocks, and unusual curio cabinets, as well as mantel pieces with collections are often displayed. Any or all of the items may be stolen or be consumed in a fire and pictures will help when filing a claim for compensation.

Follow the same procedure for every room in the house. Make notes on rooms with art pieces, gun cabinets, coin collections, sculpture, and other prized possessions. Include the attic and basement.

As you take pictures, compile a list, with room location, of all these valuables. Then, as soon as the pictures have been made, go back and engrave the items using an ID number (drivers' license is the preferred ID since it is the easiest to be traced by authorities). Items to small for the full number should be given some sort of individualistic mark in case you ever need to make positive identification. Do not use social security numbers alone - it is difficult for anyone other than yourself to get information about them. Burglars often pass up items with ID numbers engraved - they find it hard to sell easily identified goods and know that some buyers are ever on alert for stolen goods. You should also list serial numbers of items: TV's, guns, cameras, etc. You now have a list of pictures with an ID number for all pictured items. Make a machine copy or two of your lists and put in a safe place with a set of pictures. The original list should go in your safe deposit box or in some place away from the house along with a set of the pictures.

It is suggested you make copies of all your valuable papers and store the originals. This will prevent their loss in the event of fire, flood, vandalism, or burglary. It is also a good idea to have copies of daily used documents such as drivers' license, credit cards, and other ID's. It helps when you need replacements.

While taking pictures for security purposes, take your time and make notes on the safety of the premises. A number of housekeeping items should be examined and corrections made where necessary.

FLOOR COVERINGS

Look carefully at rugs, carpets, runners, and other floor coverings. If any are loose, they may cause a slip and a fall. A curling edge can trip you. Repairs to backing or renewal of adhesives may be needed. Do not take chances - get them repaired. Falls are always serious, and to the senior citizen, they may be fatal. If telephone or electrical extension cords are positioned under carpets or rugs, make sure they are properly anchored. It is better to have all such cords routed along or behind baseboards for aesthetic as well as safety purposes.

TELEPHONES

All telephone outlets should have prominently displayed numbers for fire stations, police departments, poison centers, ambulance services, and other emergency services along with emergency numbers for all utilities. The numbers should be large enough to read without glasses. In fire or other emergency situations, we don't always have the time to look for spectacles! Telephones in Senior Citizens homes should be in low enough positions to reached from floor level. Injuries from a fall may prevent you from getting up to a wall phone or a phone resting on a high counter.

SMOKE DETECTORS

Smoke detectors must be properly located and in working order if they are to do their job. A minimum of one smoke detector per floor, installed as per manufacturers instructions, is a must. They should be placed near bedrooms on ceilings (or on walls six to twelve inches below the ceiling) and away from air vents. A smoke detector in the basement and one in the attic are safeguards every home needs. And - after the smoke detectors are installed, make up a regular inspection routine and follow it to make sure batteries and bulbs are working and detector grilles are clean.

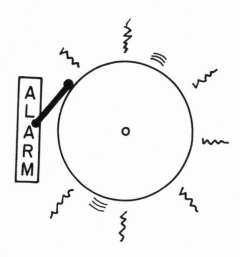

ELECTRICAL OUTLETS AND LIGHTS

All electrical outlets and switches need to be checked at regular intervals by sight and by touch. A sight inspection will reveal obvious defects and touching switches or outlets will detect any unusual warmth that may tell of faulty wiring. Any defective switch or outlet should be removed from service until an electrician has checked them out. Do not try to repair switches or outlets in place - ordinary 110 volt current can kill!

Senior Citizens are often guilty of attempts to compensate for failing eyesight by the use of extra wattage light bulbs. This can lead to fires caused by overheating. Recessed lights, ceiling fixtures, and hooded lamps trap and hold heat. Always use 60 watt bulbs until you learn the correct wattage.

SPACE HEATERS

Space heaters are not desirable for home heating purposes. However, many are in use, and if you use them, use them properly. More home fires are caused by space heaters than anything else outside of the kitchen area. Place them so they cannot be easily upset. Keep them away from flammable materials. Do not use them in halls or other passageways. Make sure they are a safe distance from furniture, drapes, curtains, and carpets. If they must be used in carpeted areas - put a poor heat conducting barrier under them.

Most electric heaters have a three pronged plug. The third prong is designed to reduce the risk of electrical shock. If your wall receptacle has only two openings, use an adapter to accept the three prong plug before using any appliance, especially a space heater.

Space heaters fueled by gas, fuel oil, or kerosene require some type of venting system. The venting system must be checked at regular intervals with considerable frequency. If a space heater must be used on a temporary basis in an unvented area, the room doors and windows should be left partially open. Senior Citizens are at special risk to poisoning from carbon monoxide

If space heaters must be used in your house, and you do not know exactly how to properly install them, call the nearest fire department. They know what to do and are always willing to give assistance.

OTHER HEATING

If you heat, completely or partially, with woodburning stoves or fireplaces, know they need special attention. Certain local building codes must be met when using woodstoves, and this applies to installation and operation. Stove chimneys need to be taken apart and cleaned after each season. A fireproof barrier between the woodstove and floor is an absolute requirement.

Fireplaces should have fire screens and proper draft so smoke does not back from the flue. All chimneys must be kept free of leaves and other debris. A cover for the chimney during warm seasons will keep dirt, bats, stray wildlife, and birds out of the house and prevent mosquitoes from using it as a passageway into the house.

An annual cleaning is recommended for all fireplaces prior to the first use of the season. Buildings can settle and cracks can open in the best built chimney. Other safety tips for fireplace owners are:

1. If you don't use the fireplace every week, check to be sure something hasn't nested in there during the idle period.

2. Do not burn processed wood or plywood - released chemicals may be dangerous.

3. Do not burn paper - the ashes can cause roof fires, and if creosote deposits are present, you could have a chimney fire.

4. Burning plastic is forbidden. Fumes are dangerous.

5. Creosote buildup comes from oak - pine burns clean.

6. Using firelighters or commercial logs or dry kindling is best for starting fires.

Stop the survey at this point. Check all the items you have examined. Ask yourself the following questions (and hope you have the answers).

1. Is the front door at least 1-1/4 inches thick of solid material with a wide angle (peep hole) lens, a deadbolt, and covered hinges?

2. Are all valuables engraved and listed with list ready to be stored in a safe place with pictures?

3. Are floor coverings securely tacked or glued with electrical and telephone wires anchored and in good repair?

4. Are emergency numbers near the telephone in large print, and is one telephone placed low enough to be reached from floor level?

5. Are smoke detectors (in number and properly installed) in place with working batteries and lights?

6. Are electrical outlets and switches in

good repair, and are all light bulbs of proper wattage?

7. Are electric space heaters properly placed and grounded, and are fuel type space heaters vented and properly placed?

8. Do woodburning stoves and fireplaces meet safety requirements?

THE KITCHEN SURVEY

The favorite room in a house, in prose, in poetry, and in fact, is the kitchen. It rates especially high with Senior Citizens. Pictured and storied as a warm and cozy nook, it is also the room in which most house fires begin.

A number of things need to be studied with great care in the kitchen area: the range area, the lighting, the ventilation, appliances, and outlets used to operate them - and most of all- the type and location of the fire extinguisher.

Your range is the point from which most fires begin. Factors that contribute include flammable items left on or near the burners. Towels, curtains, cleaning rags, oven mitts, and plastic handled kitchen tools are among the most common. Never leave any flammable item on your range. Gas ranges have pilot lights burning in most instances and this tiny flame can ignite a number of vapors and liquids used in the household. The use of flammable cleaning or other liquids in a kitchen where gas pilots are lighted may be dangerous.

Most kitchens have vents leading to the outside of the house to exhaust fumes, prevent build up of gases, and remove pollutants. These vents need to be cleaned on a regular basis. Grease may build up in them leading to a flash fire or explosion. If a ventilation system fails to operate properly, open windows and/or doors until smoke and vapors are eliminated.

Electrical appliances should not be used near the sink area. The chance of grounding with moisture present cannot be ignored. It is unwise to use appliances over heated surfaces. Heat may melt plastic parts or delicate transistors causing them to short out and possibly harm the user, and certainly damage the appliance. Extension cords should not be used in kitchens except in emergencies. If they are used, they should be confined by wiring guides. If you do not have enough electrical outlets in your kitchen, have new outlets installed. Make sure new outlets have ground fault circuit interrupter (GFCI's) to protect users against electrical shock.

Lighting in kitchens should be bright without glare. Poor lighting may be the cause of cuts and burns. Lights and light fixtures should have correct wattage bulbs. If correct wattage needed is not known, use a 60 watt bulb until correct wattage is known.

An updated and proper type of fire extinguisher must be in every kitchen! To have otherwise is gambling with your life. Grease fires and other kinds of fires can be contained if immediate action is taken. Call your fire department for information on the size and type of fire extinguisher they recommend for your kitchen. Never forget - most house fires start in the kitchen.

Inspect all cabinets in the kitchen. If light is needed, areas under kitchen cabinets are good places to install additional light fixtures. Cabinet doors should have some type of automatic closures. Cabinet doors left open cause numerous eye injuries, skinned heads and broken noses.

After a final glance at your kitchen, think about posting a sign to the effect no one will be allowed to use the range or oven while wearing clothing with baggy sleeves. The U.S. Consumer Product Safety Commission estimates *seventy (70%) percent of all people who die from clothing fires are 65 years of age or older* - and most of them catch their clothing on fire in the kitchen.

Bathrobes, kimonos, coats, long sleeved sweaters, and nightgowns catch pot handles, skillet handles, and pan covers causing them to overturn inflicting severe burns, scalding, and often, fires.

If the ban on baggy sleeves is ignored, perhaps it will alert users to roll up sleeves or tie them down with rubber bands to reduce their potential danger.

Again, stop your survey at this point. You should be able to answer these with a "yes", or "action to be taken as soon as possible".

1. Did I take pictures of everything in the kitchen?
2. Is the range uncluttered and is it vented with clean vents?
3. Are there plenty of outlets, away from the sink, for appliances?
4. Is lighting in the kitchen sufficiently bright without glare?
5. Is a fire extinguisher of the correct type and updated present?
6. Is a sign forbidding floppy sleeves at the range and oven posted?
7. Do cabinet doors have automatic closers?
8. Are outlets equipped with ground fault interrupters (GFCI's)?
9. Is the kitchen floor free of water and grease?

BATHROOM SAFETY

The most dangerous room in the house, except for the fire hazards in the kitchen, is the bathroom. Thousands of deaths are caused each year by people falling in bathrooms, people being electrocuted, people being scalded, people being drowned, and people being poisoned by taking the wrong medicine or mistaking other materials for medicine.

In order to make this most private (privacy contributes to the death rate in bathrooms) of rooms

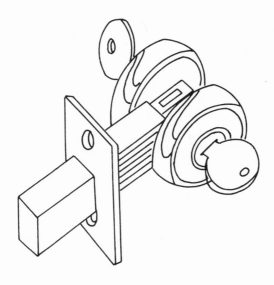

in the house safer, it requires close attention to a number of items, and some additional work. Check each item with care.

The floor of the bathroom should have a non-skid surface. Moisture on tile or other surfaces without non-skid treatment can cause falls. Senior Citizens are most susceptible due to lack of agility. A fall in a bathroom is extremely dangerous because of the hardness and contours of bathtubs, lavatories, and toilets.

Mats, high grade textured strips or appliques in the shower stall and the tub are highly recommended. Rubber or plastic mats are a second choice, if used alone, because they may slip if not carefully placed so the suction disks on the bottom take hold.

Every tub and shower should have at least two grab bars installed. They not only help prevent falling, but they are an assistance to getting into and out of the water safely. Present grab bars and future installations should be tested for strength and ease of use. Grab bars attached through walls into structural supports are the safest. There are special bars designed to be attached to the sides of bathtubs. You should make a note of sliding doors used around tubs and showers as to ease of operation and any sharp edges along the door or its track. Cuts and pinched appendages from poorly installed or manufactured shower and tub sliding doors are a common occurrence.

Lights in bathrooms should be controlled from a switch near the door. Switches that glow in the dark are desirable. A night light plugged into an outlet near the floor may prevent a stumble in the dark. Seniors are more frequent users of bathroom facilities at night than others. Entering the bathroom usually without eyeglasses, is an extra hazard they face. It is an area which requires careful pre-planning or upgrading of facilities. Use correct wattage bulbs, and if proper wattage is not known, use 60 watt bulbs pending certainty.

Senior Citizens often forget the effort needed to make muscles perform the simple acts of standing and sitting. The loss of muscle power is an ongoing situation and the acknowledgement of this loss has prompted inventors and others to find and market items to make bathrooms safer. Shower safety stools with non-skid tips are available. Elevated toilet seats and toilets surrounded by safety frames to be used with previously recommended grab bars help make the bathroom a safer room.

Check the hot water heater thermostat. Although it is probably not located in the bathroom, it has an important part in making the bathroom safer. Scalding is a major cause of injury to Senior Citizens. By setting the thermostat to not more than 120 degrees fahrenheit, many scalding cases can be avoided. It will also save you money. Installation of a thermostatic mixing valve is an added safety feature. However - it is always wise to test water temperature by hand before getting into a tub or turning a shower on full force.

Almost every bathroom has a cabinet of some type - usually hanging just over the lavatory. It is commonly called - and used for - a medicine cabinet. Physicians and pharmacists are recommending keeping all medications elsewhere. They note the high humidity in the bathroom causes medicines to lose their effectiveness in a very short period of time. Plus, they know how many of us reach for a container, gulp a dose from it without looking and wind up having to have our stomachs pumped! It is better to have dosages separated and placed on a night table, with a glass of water.

It is worth noting that our beloved grandchildren often climb up to the "medicine cabinet" and sample the contents. They are unable to read labels and often cannot identify which "candy" they took and become casualties.

Medicines do no good unless used as prescribed. Many drugs become poisons if improperly used. Label all medicines with letters easy to read, giving dosages, time to use, and the expiration date of effectiveness. Along with the name of the person taking medications should be a list of all medical allergies, blood type, and any physical problems.

The use of electrical appliances in bathrooms - hair dryers, water picks, shavers, curling irons, etc. - is common - and can be dangerous. An appliance plugged into a socket can become deadly if it falls into water. Never attempt to remove an appliance from water until it has been unplugged! Bathrooms furnish excellent grounding, and electrocution is a common cause of bathroom deaths. Of all places in the home, ground faulty interrupters (GFCI's) are most needed here.

One last security tip about the bathroom. Although it is the most private of rooms, carefully consider doing without locking doors. A sign indicating occupancy on the outside should suffice and, certainly, will not impede any necessary rescue attempts. If you fall, faint, choke, or become otherwise incapacitated, you are in enough trouble without being locked in! Think about it - your welfare is more important than any embarrassment that you might suffer because you forgot to post your sign.

We, again, stop our survey to ask ourselves the following:

1. Do we have pictures of the bathroom?
2. Are non-skid mats or strips in the tub and shower?
3. Are grab bars installed in shower and tub area?
4. Is the light switch near the door? Does it glow in the dark?
5. Is hot water heater thermostat set at a maximum of 120 degrees?
6. Are shower stools, elevated toilet seats, and frames in place?
7. Are lights bright and is a night light in place?
8. Have ground fault circuit interrupters (GFCI's) been installed?
9. Has a decision as to where to keep the medications been made?

BEDROOM SURVEY

With camera on ready - we move into the bedroom areas. Each bedroom should receive close scrutiny with most attention being paid to the master bedroom.

Bedrooms are used for sleeping rooms, reading rooms, and often hold other items such as curio cabinets with collections, trophy cases, and all sorts of sewing materials. All items need to be pictured and inventoried, as do beds, chests of drawers, cedar chests, and other valuable furniture.

The first thing to check are the floor coverings. As was done in the living room, make sure rugs, carpets, mats, throw rugs, and the like are firmly anchored.

The areas immediately adjacent to beds need special attention for Seniors. Readily available lamps with easy to operate switches, night lights, and a flashlight for each occupant within reach is recommended. Seniors are subject to rising during the night, and they need adequate lighting.

Smoking is detrimental to your health at all times, but when done in bed - it is deadly. One half of all deaths caused from mattress and other bedding fires are suffered by Senior Citizens! And - the majority of these fires are started by those who smoke in bed. **DON'T SMOKE** is the first security measure to take when making the golden years safer years - but if you must - **NEVER SMOKE IN BED!**

Use electric blankets as per manufacturers instructions. The sides of electric blankets "tucked in" with ends "folded over" causes fires. The extra blankets piled on top of electric blankets are not needed and are fire hazards.

Heating pads are a blessing to many of us with sore muscles and bones that need warmth, but they must be turned off before we go to sleep. Severe burns from heating pads may be caused from active heating pads, and they are often the source of fires.

A telephone in the bedroom can be valuable in the event of an emergency. The bell can be turned off or lowered if desired. An answering machine can pick up night messages if needed. If your area has a 911 system, that's the only number you will need - otherwise have emergency numbers in large print near the bedroom telephone.

After checking each bedroom in the house, ask these questions:

1. Have all valuable items and furniture been pictured?

2. Are floor coverings firmly anchored and electrical cords secured?

3. Are household members and guests forbidden to smoke in bed?

4. Are electric blankets and heating pads properly used?

5. Is a telephone handy?

SPECIAL PARAGRAPH

Keeping a firearm in the bedroom, or any room, for protection against intruders is a personal matter you must decide for yourself. The author is a member of the National Rifle Association and has handled firearms for a number of years. He feels safer with his weapon within easy reach. The weapon is secured each time he leaves the house so unauthorized persons or children cannot handle it. If you keep a firearm for protection, be sure you know how to care for it and how to use it properly.

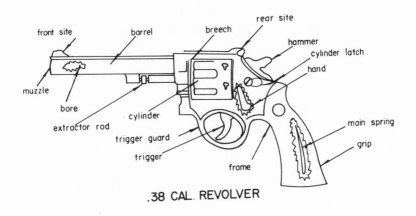

.38 CAL. REVOLVER

If in doubt, write the N.R.A. for information or call your local law enforcement agency. Many firing ranges work with Senior Citizens in handling firearms with safety.

SURVEY OF STEPS AND STAIRWAYS

Houses with steps and/or stairways may cause problems for Senior Citizens. Our aged and aging bones grow brittle with time and break more easily. Broken bones in Senior Citizens often lead to more serious complications. In view of this, we must be extra cautious when climbing stairways and when coming back down. It is best to have at least one or two hand railings for every flight of steps and/or stairs. The treads should have good coverings in good repair and all steps/stairways should be well lighted.

Any railings installed should be firmly anchored the full length of the stairway or steps. Construction materials should be smooth to the touch but not slippery. Railings must provide a firm handhold.

To check for correct lighting, look down at the tread when you go up and again when you come down a flight. If you can see the edges of the steps clearly, lighting is O.K. The use of indirect lighting or frosted bulbs will reduce shadows and glare. Light switches should be at the top and the bottom of each stairway so they never have to be used in darkness. If a switch is not at the top and bottom of your stairways, you should have them installed without delay.

Treads on stairways should have firmly attached non-skid carpeting kept clean and in good condition inside the house. Outside steps and stairways should have abrasive strips and/or textured paint to prevent slipping.

Risers and treads should be even, with the same distance for each step. If any steps deviate from the pattern in width or height, mark them and make corrections as soon as possible.

Before leaving the subject of steps and stairways - a reminder that nothing should ever be left, even temporarily, on steps. A fall while climbing or coming down steps can be fatal.

STAIRWAY AND STEP CHECKLIST

1. Have pictures been taken of steps and stairways been taken showing upward, downward, and side views?
2. Are stairways well lighted with shadows and glares eliminated?
3. Are treads in good condition with firmly fastened carpeting?
4. Do outside stairways have adhesive strips or textured paint?
5. Are risers and treads even with identical distances for each?
6. Are light switches present at top and bottom of stairways?

STORAGE OF DANGEROUS ITEMS

We seem to forever have a number of dangerous items around the house: gasoline for mowers, bug killers, paints, fuel oil, toilet cleaners, and many others.

Each of these potentially hazardous items must be properly stored. The first step is to make sure containers are tightly closed when we have finished using them - temporarily or permanently. Containers must not leak vapors or liquids. All containers should be stored away from areas with flames or high heat build up. Many chemicals, and especially the gasoline used for power equipment such as mowers, powers saws and edgers, are very volatile. They may be touched off by arcs from electrical switches. Gasoline fumes have been ignited from gas hot water heaters more than twenty feet away. Many insurance companies refuse to pay claims on fires that have been proved to have been ignited from improperly stored flammable materials.

Before storing any hazardous material, label and use a safety container. Make and keep a list of materials stored in your storage area. Check all fuels before re-filling equipment tanks - the wrong fuel use can lead to disaster. If labels become unreadable on chemicals, dispose of them. Improper use of chemicals can be deadly.

CHECKLIST OF STORED ITEMS

1. Are all containers sealed and tightly closed?

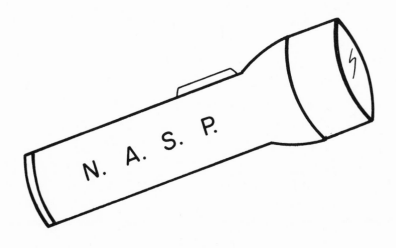

2. Are all items stored away from flames or heat build up areas?

3. Are all container labels legible and in place?

4. Is it necessary to have these materials on hand?

SURVEY OF BASEMENTS, GARAGES, AND WORK AREAS

Many houses do not have basements, garages, or work shops, but for those that do, security and safety precautions are a necessity.

Often the basement and/or the garage area does double duty, serving as a work area in addition to its original use intent. When this is true, extra caution should be exercised.

Garages and work shops have an ever present housekeeping hazard resulting from the careless discarding of greasy rags and cloths. They are sources of fires from spontaneous combustion. All greasy rags and cloths should be dropped into a metal container and removed from the work area when work is interrupted.

Another common danger in the work area is the accumulation of sawdust, wood shavings, and metal filings. The work area should be thoroughly cleaned at the end of the days work. A fire from any cause can feed on leftovers on the work shop floor, and if you fall, the metal filings can cause serious injury. Before you start a new project - clean up after the old one first.

Most work shops have a number of extension cords available. These should be examined for wear and repaired or discarded. The 110 volts in the average work shop - or the 220 volts installed in some - are killers when improperly handled. All power tools, including their cords, must be equipped with three pronged plugs in order to ground them and keep them safe for use. If it is absolutely necessary to use a three pronged plug in a two hole outlet, use a three pronged adapter until outlets can be changed.

Fuse or circuit breaker boxes should have all circuits clearly marked as to which individual areas they furnish power. This information will allow you to cut power from a circuit needing repairs, etc. without disturbing other power in the house. If the house uses fuses, a supply of correct sized fuses should be on hand for replacements. *Using a penny in the socket of a blown fuse is utter foolishness.* Fuses burn out to warn of trouble, and if we circumvent the system, we invite fire or other disaster. Modern houses are almost always equipped with circuit breaker panels making it easy to flip a switch when trouble appears on lines.

Work shop areas, basements, and garages should be well lighted without shadows and/or glaring from lights. Shop equipment, pipes, tools, materials, and other items make for easy tripping and falling. Each of these areas should have switches near entrances and exits and should never be entered without having the lights on. If power is off, a flashlight should be used. It is best to have emergency lights with battery operation strategically placed for protection in the event of sudden power loss. A rechargeable flashlight inserted at constant charge in an outlet near the door is recommended if emergency lights are not present.

Power tools are unforgiving of improper use. Senior Citizens must be extra careful when handling them. Safety guards must be in place and good working order. Ground fault circuit interrupters (GFCI's) should be on each tool. The thousands of Senior Citizens treated at emergency rooms each year is testament to the dangers of using power tools without great care.

A correctly sized fire extinguisher of the proper type should be positioned where it can be easily reached in garages, basements, and work shops of all houses, and it must be serviced at regular intervals.

No smoking signs posted with strict observance of the rule is a must in basements, garages, and work shops. The ease of a fire starting in these areas and the difficulty of controlling fires in these areas is tremendous. If you must smoke - step outside.

CHECKLIST FOR BASEMENTS, GARAGES AND WORKSHOPS

1. Are floors cleared of sawdust, metal filings, and wood shavings?
2. Are metal containers used for greasy rags and cloths until disposal?
3. Are extension cords in good repair?
4. Do all power tools have three pronged plugs?

5. Are electrical outlets equipped with three holes?
6. If fused - are extra fuses nearby?
7. Are all circuits from breaker box properly labelled?
8. Are areas shadow and glare free with proper wattage bulbs?
9. Are ground fault circuit interrupters (GFCI's) and power tool guards in place?
10. Is a light switch at entrances and exits with a flashlight nearby?
11. Is an updated fire extinguisher of proper type and first aid kit handy?

EMERGENCY EXIT PLAN

After you have completed the survey of the exterior and interior of your house, the final step for the house proper is to prepare an emergency exit plan. It need not be elaborate, but it must take into consideration all exigencies. Everyone living in the house must be familiar with the plan. It is also very wise to acquaint overnight visitors with the plan. The plan should cover any type of emergency. Whatever situation arises of an emergency nature, time will probably be in short supply, and - in most emergencies - confusion reigns. So - the for the first entry at the top of the emergency plan - in extra large letters - write **DO NOT PANIC!** More lives are lost and people hurt in emergencies due to panic than any other factor.

To begin the exit plan, designate the number of exits available. In fire situations, an exit or exits may be at or near the point of the fire and impossible to use. Senior Citizens slowed by their years must study all exits and determine if they are physically able to utilize them. It may be extremely difficult to try and clamber out of a window.

After deciding the number and kind of exits to be used, a place outside of the house should be selected as the point where all occupants are to assemble immediately upon escaping the building. This will allow anyone still trying to escape the building to receive help from those already outside and prevent anyone from returning to the building searching for someone already clear. After the plan has been completed, and written down, for study and to show others who may move in or visit, make a practice run. Every member of the household should take part in the practice run. The time it takes the slowest member of the household to evacuate the house from the most distant part of the house and arrive at the designated gathering point will set the maximum evacuation time to be expected. Then - in an actual emergency - anyone absent after the maximum allowable time will signal the others that a rescue party is needed. Knowing the exit plan will allow the rescuers to find you in the shortest period of time.

EMERGENCY EXIT PLAN CHECKLIST

1. Has the plan been written with all householders present?
2. Does the plan include emergencies due to fire, storms, and all disasters?
3. Is more than a single exit designated?
4. Has a meeting point for those leaving the house been selected?
5. Have practice runs been held and slowest time of members been recorded?

Commit this emergency exit plan to memory. Make sure everyone knows exactly what their part in the plan is and then hold unscheduled practices of the exit plan at least four times per year. Practices are necessary for all members of the household and should be accomplished without warning just as emergency situations arise.

THE YARD

Other than for the driveway and sidewalk areas, yard security and safety has not been addressed other than to ask you to determine positions for placement of outside flood lights and how much the shrubbery needs to be trimmed. The reason is that the subject is so large, it was decided it should be addressed in the chapter entitled "AT PLAY".

FENCES

Fences in residential areas prompt would be intruders to seek easier entry and departure paths. A good grade chain link fence with gates secured by steel locks is a barrier noticed by those who wish easy and non-noticed approach. The fence indicates a watch dog may be present. Combined with good lighting, fences are a deterrent.

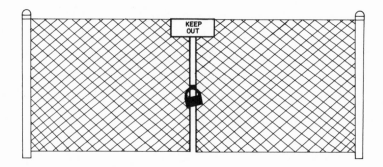

ALARM SYSTEMS

The marketplace has a number of simple to highly sophisticated alarm systems available to homeowners. Some operate on movement sensors, some on heat sensors, some on mechanical detection, and many provide accompanying siren or other noise producing accessories. Since they are constantly being upgraded and require expert installation, they will not be discussed herein. A phone call will get you the latest information and assistance. Just be sure you call a reputable firm and check the license and ID of any sales or installation personnel.

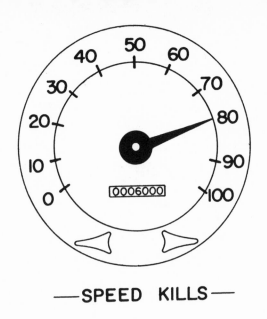

—SPEED KILLS—

Chapter 3
THE AUTOMOBILE

To own an automobile has become an American tradition. Most Senior Citizens have owned a number of them. We have driven them since age 16 and will drive them until we can no longer see the road. We are survivors of one of the most dangerous activities on earth - getting behind the wheel of an automobile and driving it.

We know statistics show more deaths from traffic in any given recent year than for a similar period in any of our wars. We have lost friends and perhaps relatives in automobile "accidents" (We know accidents don't happen - they are caused). We also know of numerous incidents where those who did not die were left crippled.

In spite of this knowledge, we fail to practice good driving habits. Our automobile has become such a part of us we do things automatically. We slide through stop signs. We fail to "stop, look, and listen" at railroad crossings. We do not see signal lights change. We change traffic lanes without giving a signal and many times fail to look before changing. We look right, then look left, then pull into moving lanes of cars without looking either way again. We drive over the speed limit imposed by law.

We drive after taking medication. We are guilty of playing the suicidal game of "having one for the road" then climbing under the steering wheel.

Many of us move to different states, and unless the state requires us to take an examination to get a new license, we don't know how their driving laws differ from those we've been accustomed to obeying.

Few of us have had a day of formal driving education. It wasn't required in our youth - we learned from friend or relative. However - most of us could use a refresher course. It will help us get rid of some of the bad driving habits we have accumulated.

We realize our reflexes are slower. Our feet do not ease off accelerators and reach brakes as quickly. Our vision is not as sharp. We have lost some ability to judge distances. Our hearing has been dulled. With radio or tape playing and air conditioner humming, we roll along in the extra quiet of modern automobiles lulled into a false sense of security.

LEARNING TO DRIVE

Many Senior Citizens have never learned to drive. They have depended upon someone else for transportation. The someone has usually been a relative or spouse. Then one day, circumstances take away this someone. If you do not know how to drive and are physically able, make arrangements to learn how to drive as soon as possible. Driving schools are available in both public and private areas.

In our society, transportation systems are based on the automobile, and non-drivers pay a heavy penalty for not having learned this relatively simple task.

AUTO SAFETY

Driving with faulty brakes, worn tires, weathered windshield wipers, non-operating horn, leaking muffler, or other mechanical deficiency is courting danger. Take advantage of one of the many free inspection offers advertised, making sure you are allowed to be present at all points of inspection. After the inspection, any "needs to be done" list should be taken to either another of these inspection offers or to a mechanic of your choice. Some "free" offers are rip-offs and border on fraud. Always get a second opinion.

We seldom find the "service" station we once knew. We pump our own gasoline, check our own oil level, and put air in our tires. We can't operate without periodically taking on gasoline, but many of us neglect the air in our tires and fail to check the oil often enough. If you aren't up to doing these maintenance items, stop at least once a month at a full service station and watch closely as each of these tasks are completed. While you are there, ask for a check of radiator coolant/anti-freeze, all drive belts, battery connections, power steering and brake fluids. Most automobile breakdowns can be traced to poor maintenance.

Read the owners' manual on your vehicle and have it serviced regularly as per instructions at an authorized dealer or by your own mechanic. If your automobile lets you down on the open road - your life may be at stake!!!

EQUIPMENT

As a senior citizen, you remember when your new car came with a set of tools. They came in a metal box with some models and wrapped in fabric with individual tool loops in others. Those days are apparently gone forever - but we need a few essential tools for emergency situations.

It is a good idea to have fundamental knowledge of how each tools should be used. You may not have the expertise or strength to use them, but your knowledge may help someone who is assisting you. (The author hit a broken bottle in the road several years ago, causing a flat tire. A young man stopped and offered help but did not know what to do. The lug wrench that came with the car was so flimsy it twisted with the first attempt to remove a lug nut. A senior lady stopped and loaned a solid lug wrench from her car. The young man, following instructions, soon had the wheel off and the spare tire in place. My knowledge and the young man's strength put me back on the road.)

Every motorist should have a good jack in the auto. It should be strong enough to lift the car easily.

Also recommended is a piece of scrap wood (2"x 8") a foot long to support the jack in loose soil and a brick or similar object to prevent the car from rolling. A can containing air and puncture sealing material purchased from your local department store auto department is a wise addition to your trunk.

A small tool kit with pliers, end wrenches, screwdrivers, knife, can of lubricating oil, and an extra quart of engine oil with an assortment of bolts and nuts and a roll of both electrical and friction tape may come in handy.

The automobile of today does not start when pushed. You probably haven't seen a crank in many years. The only way to start our modern engines is with electrical power from a battery. Fortunately, we can borrow battery power from another battery by using "jumper cables". These cables are rubber or plastic covered copper wires used to carry current from one battery to another, supplying the weak battery with enough cranking power to start the engine. You should carry a set of jumper cables in the trunk of your car. You never know when an electrical short, leaving the lights on after a rain, or other incident is going to severely weaken your battery.

When purchasing jumper cables, insist on heavy gauge (#4 or #6) wire. Light wire may not carry enough current to start an engine. Study the instructions before using jumper cables. Clamp positive and negative clamps on the good battery at one end. Then, clamp the positive clamp on the other end to the positive post of the weaker battery. The negative clamp goes to a metal spot on the frame of the weak battery car. By running the engine of the car with the good battery a few minutes, you build up a charge in the weak battery which combines with the power of the good battery to start the engine. After starting the engine, remove the clamp from the engine frame first. This prevents sparking that might ignite acid fumes from a battery which might cause an explosion. Over 25,000 individuals suffer damage to their eyes each year from exploding batteries.

Another item you should have in your car is a one or two gallon gas container of approved material with a flexible nozzle. ***Do not carry gasoline in your car!!*** It can be disastrous in an accident. A container will make it convenient when you locate a supply if you run out of fuel. You should carry at least one quart of proper weight oil in an easy to open container for emergency situations.

A few newspapers, a drop cloth or plastic tarp, a pair of cotton work gloves, a roll of paper towels, and a pair of coveralls take up little trunk space and are handy in case of road trouble as are safety flares and a fire extinguisher.

Many auto clubs offer towing and road services to members and most have other benefits such as trip planning, etc. AARP has been a leader in this field for years - write them.

AUTO CHECKLIST

1. Test the horn, turn signals, and bright and dim headlights.
2. Check the brakes, tires, windshield wipers, and muffler.
3. Check or have checked all fluids, including radiator coolant, power steering, brake and battery, transmission, and crankcase fluids.
4. Check drive belts and battery connections.
5. Make sure your trunk has a good jack with supports and wheel chocks, a good lug wrench, and a can of air and puncture sealer.
6. Get #4 or #6 gauge wire jumper cables, a one or two gallon fuel container, safety flares, a tow rope or chain, and a fire extinguisher.

DRIVE BUCKLED UP!

Each time you get under the wheel of your auto or take a seat in one, BUCKLE UP! Most accidents occur within 25 miles of home base - and - on dry roads in good weather!

The U.S. Department of Transportation estimates one in three persons will have a disabling injury from an automobile accident during their lifetime. A million Americans are seriously injured in auto accidents each year and *fifty thousand more are killed!* If everyone used seat belts, these figures could be reduced by at least one third!!!

Accident studies show Senior Citizens have

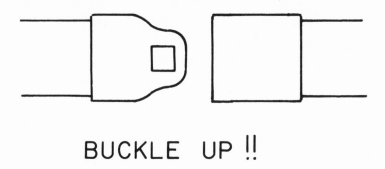

BUCKLE UP !!

less accidents than juniors, but the senior has the higher accident rate per mile driven. The elderly are more apt to be injured or killed in automobile accidents due to fragile bones and reduced ability to shake off the trauma of an accident.

Many states now have laws requiring us to "BUCKLE UP". When we were younger, there were no such laws, and we are not in the habit of using these life saving straps. A look at some of the ways these safety mechanisms work may prompt more of us to use them.

Safety Belts

    A. Provide a "ride down" effect. This means as the momentum of a car decreases in a crash, the seat belt slows the momentum of the wearer and reduces force at the point of impact. When the belt isn't fastened, the vehicle stops, but the person doesn't and flesh receives the full force of the impact.

B. Helps driver keep control of vehicle by keeping him/her behind the wheel, giving greater control.
C. Distributes force of impact across strongest parts of the body.
D. Prevents driver from hitting steering wheel, dash, windows, and windshield.
E. Prevents occupants from hitting one another at point of impact.
F. Keeps wearer from being thrown from vehicle. (You are 25 times as likely to suffer fatal injury if you are thrown from a vehicle).

DRIVING TIPS

As soon as you enter your vehicle, lock all doors and roll up windows to a point that prevents anyone from reaching in - keep them that way.

Travel well-lighted and busy streets if possible. Avoid areas known to be dangerous.

Never Pick Up Hitchhikers!!!

Pass up stranded motorists but notify police of the location. Being "stranded" is a ruse used by many criminals.

Mentally note places like police and fire stations, gasoline stations, and stores on regular routes you travel - in an emergency, knowing such locations might save you.

IF YOUR VEHICLE IS DISABLED

No one is exempt from flat tires, running out of fuel or mechanical troubles. We do not anticipate them, but we should always be ready if and when they occur. Recommended actions include:

1. Drive off the roadway and out of traffic.
2. Turn on emergency flashers -set flares if you have them - place the reverse side of your sun shield requesting help where it can be seen.
3. Lift the hood - tie handkerchief or red flag to radio aerial or to door handle on traffic side.
4. In case of fire, use the extinguisher.
5. If possible, stay in your car. Keep doors locked and windows up.
6. If anyone stops to help, stay in the car and ask them to call a wrecker or the police. *Do Not Go With Them.*
7. **DO NOT PANIC!** A calm head keeps control.
8. If someone else is disabled, note location

and call it in at the first opportunity. *Do not stop to help* - it may be a trap.

PARKING

When parking in an attended garage or lot, leave only the entry and ignition key, and only if required. Keys can be duplicated quickly, and with your license number, your residence is easily located. Anyone with a key to your house has an extra easy target. Look at the attendant long enough for a possible future identification and log the time and date of your parking. The information could be important in case of damage to your car, fire at the garage, or a future burglary.

If your home has a garage with garage door opener - raise and lower the door when entering the driveway. You may scare off a burglar or thief, and it is better not to confront them.

Always lock the garage door and keep it locked. Burglars may enter an unlocked garage and hide until a later time. If you park in the driveway or use a carport - keep your car locked at all times.

When parking outside - at home - or away - always lock your car, even for short periods of time. Experienced thieves can "hot wire" a car in minutes. Juveniles sometimes steal an unlocked car to "joy ride" and wind up becoming criminals. Do not put temptation in front of anyone.

If possible, park under a light, night or day. You may be gone longer than planned, and it also makes it easier to find your parking spot.

Park as close to your destination as is possible, preferably on the entrance side.

Do not leave valuables on the seat in sight. If you must leave them, put them in the trunk. However, look around, many thieves watch such movements and easily pop open most trunk lids. The author, when forced to use the trunk, places valuables in the trunk before arriving at the parking space.

Park on a slope or elevated area if possible. Many lots have poor drainage, and water collects in a hurry when it rains.

If registration papers must be kept in the vehicle, use copies rather than originals. Makes it more difficult to sell the vehicle.

ENTERING YOUR VEHICLE

Any time you start to enter your car or truck, check possible spots where an intruder might hide. Back seats, bodies of pickups, and under the car on the side opposite the driver's side are favorites of criminals. If you are going to your car after dark, take your flashlight.

CAR THEFT PREVENTION TIPS

Over a million automobiles are stolen each year in the U.S. They are stolen from driveways, mall parking areas, from streets, parking garages, and many other places.

The reasons for stealing, to mention a few, are:

joy rides, temporary transportation, to use in other criminal acts, and to sell.

Although nothing can prevent all car theft, there are specific steps you can take to reduce the risk. Car thieves like Senior Citizens' cars because they know they are generally well cared for. Precautions may include the following:

A. Park in well lighted areas. Criminals do not like light.

B. Park with wheels turned sharply in one direction - it makes towing more difficult.

C. Always lock your car, roll the windows up, and keep the key.

D. Keep valuables out of sight - put them in the trunk.

E. When leaving a vehicle in an attended spot - do not give a time of return.

PARKING LOTS AND GARAGES

Insiders have been known to loot trunks, switch batteries, and steal other items. Check your car inside and out when you return.

Over half the vehicles stolen each year disappear forever. They wind up in "chop shops" where they are stripped for parts. They may be painted another color and sold. Many are wrecked and/or burned. Some models and makes are more likely to be stolen than others, but none are exempt.

The modern car thief has become very sophisticated. Many of them can enter, start, and drive away a car in less than two minutes.

On the other hand, crime fighters have devised a number of items to help citizens make car theft more difficult. Electronic control modules, hidden switches, special locks for hoods and trunks, alarms, and devices to warn of theft are on the market. In addition, locks for locking brake pedals to steering wheels, engine disabling switches, and electrical system cut-offs are available. Your mechanic can tell you where to obtain them.

AUTO FIRE

Fire is always a possibility. A good fire extinguisher, easy to reach and made to combat auto fires is an excellent security item. In collision situations, gasoline tanks can rupture. Unused fuel in the carburetion system may splash over hot engines. If your car is on fire or smoke starts from under the hood, get out of traffic and out of the car.

Use your extinguisher. If flames persist, move away from the car. Gasoline is highly flammable and may explode.

Prevention is the key to good security. If you smell gasoline fumes in your vehicle - check it out immediately. A leaking gasoline line can trigger a major disaster.

GUNS IN VEHICLES

Many Senior Citizens carry guns in their vehicles. If carried in a legal manner and properly safeguarded, it is an expression of independence and the exercise of rights afforded U.S. citizens by the Constitution.

However - a check with state laws, should be made before you carry a gun in your vehicle. One state may allow you to carry a gun in your car if kept in a glove compartment or under a seat where it is not immediately available for use - others may not.

If you intend to have a gun in your vehicle, possess the knowledge to operate it safely. It should be kept in good working order and the ammunition should be fresh. Guns should be hidden from view when you leave your vehicle.

Anyone who uses or expects to use a firearm should make plans to visit a firing range at regular intervals to keep in practice.

DRIVERS' LICENSES AND REGISTRATION PAPERS

Your drivers' license is also your best method of identifying yourself. The number is on file at your state motor vehicle headquarters. The number is yours for life and is readily available to law enforcement personnel. Engraving your license number on valuables such as cameras, guns, TVs, and the like makes recovery of stolen or lost items much easier. It also acts as a deterrent because many burglars do not want to risk taking objects that are easily identifiable. Keep your drivers' license on your person but make a machine copy for your valuable papers file.

Car registration papers should be copied and

originals stored with valuable papers. A copy, plainly marked "copy - not valid for transfer", will establish your ownership if needed. If your car is stolen, the copy will not allow the thief to sell your car easily.

KEYS

An extra set of car keys should be kept with valuable papers. Keys can also be used as a defensive weapon. A key held firmly between thumb and forefinger jabbed into an assailant's eyes, nose, lips, or ribs while you yell "FIRE" may buy enough time to save your life or possessions.

Keys attached to items such as Nasprotector (tm) available from the National Association of Security Personnel may also be used to ward off an assault while you yell "FIRE".

Yelling "FIRE" rather than "HELP" is advised because mankind has never lost the fear of fire and more of us pay attention to a cry of "FIRE" than to any other word.

MAPS

Having a good map and marking it is good security. Being forced to stop to ask for directions exposes you to possible danger. If you get lost, you may wind up in a dangerous neighborhood or find yourself on a deserted highway without a source of fuel. The stranded motorist is a favorite prey of the criminal.

DETOURS AND BARRICADES

You should be very cautious when encountering detour signs and barricades in non-busy areas after dark. Criminals steal detour and barricade signs and use them to divert unsuspecting traffic into places where they must stop and become vulnerable to attack.

IMPAIRED DRIVERS

You do not drink and drive. Neither do you use recreational drugs and drive. *However* - there are those that do - and they use the same roads you do! Join the R.I.D. program - Report Impaired Drivers. Erratic driving is one sign of an impaired driver. Report such drivers to law enforcement personnel - it may save the life of a driver and might save your life or the life of someone you love. M.A.D.D. - Mothers Against Drunk Drivers is another fine organization attempting to make our "golden years safer years".

FIRST AID KIT

A number of companies make first aid kits for the motorist. They are neatly packaged, contain all recommended first aid supplies and should be in your trunk. Your pharmacist will be happy to recommend the size you need and what it should contain for your particular situation.

First aid supplies are welcome at the scene of an accident either for you or someone else. In addition, skinned knuckles, insect bites, small cuts, and other injuries heal faster when promptly treated.

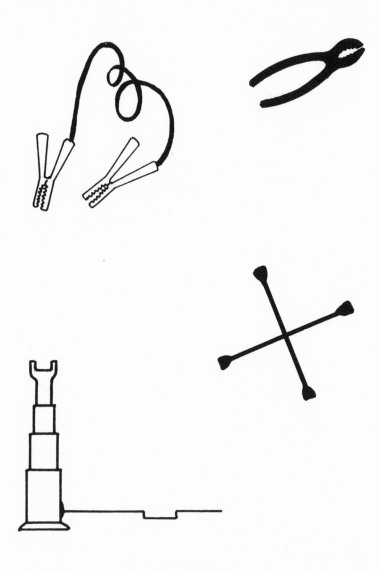

Chapter 4
THE WORKPLACE

Many of us still labor in the vineyards. Some of us because we want to, some of us because we have to. In either case, the sense of personal physical security is not what it was when we originally entered the work force. In recent years, our places of employment have joined the rest of society and have become points where dangers lurk. The robber, the burglar, the arsonist, the rapist, the drug addict, and the terrorist constantly threaten workers and the workplace.

Working men and women face the first threat to their safety when they leave home to go to work. Most of us must use some form of transportation to get to our job. Regardless of the form of transportation - we must follow good security practices while we are en route to and from work.

First - our automobile. You should never allow your gas tank to get below half capacity at the end of the day. Emergencies after dark may require considerable driving, and it may be difficult to find fuel. Time may be of the greatest essence. We can avoid bald tires easier than we can avoid bald heads. Good tires should be checked weekly for correct inflation. Brakes in good condition and an engine in good repair are necessities. If you are in a car pool, make sure insurance coverage is afforded your passengers and that you are covered as a passenger. While checking the air in your tires, check all your lights - front and rear.

If you are a subway or bus patron - take steps to make yourself more secure. Allow ample time to get to your point of departure but do not arrive a great deal ahead of time. Seniors waiting at stops are often targets of the criminal, especially females. Get to know your fellow passengers - friends are responsive.

The pick up and discharge site of your public transportation company should provide shelter in case of bad weather. It should be cleaned regularly. If you see loitering, report it to the company and the police. In congested areas, pickpockets and purse snatchers haunt loading/discharging points. Ladies must remember to keep purses close to the body with a firm grip. Men should keep wallets in an inside position - not just inside the coat.

When you drive and use parking garages or parking lots operated by commercial companies - extra caution is the word. Keep all keys except the ignition key with you. Keys are easily duplicated and you don't want your house or office keys in strange hands. Do not give attendants exact times of return. Not knowing what time you may reappear may save your car from being rifled. And - open the trunk of your car when you return, in full view of the attendant. Spare tires, tool boxes, and other items kept in trunks may be missing. If your car is damaged while in a garage or on a lot, notify the attendant and get as much information as possible before leaving. Notify your insurance company at once - they need to know. Never leave valuables on the seat where they can be seen.

ENTERING AND LEAVING THE WORKPLACE

Entrances of workplaces are other favorite hangouts of pickpockets and purse snatchers. If there are areas where potential assailants can find cover near the entrance you use, notify your director of security. Poor lighting, overgrown shrubbery, and pilasters may obstruct the view from the building and give a thief a chance to do dirty work before escaping. If different exits are used, make sure the same precautions are taken. Workers on late shift are often instructed to leave by side doors, make sure they are well-lighted.

STAIRWAYS AND ELEVATORS

Climbing stairs requires attention and use, perhaps, of handrails. Watch your step - going up or coming down steps and stairways. Debris, spilled liquids, or a loose piece of candy can cause slippery footing and a nasty fall. We are often tempted in these health conscious days to use stairwells otherwise little used. Do not enter these areas alone - rapists and robbers sometimes wait there for the unsuspecting.

Since elevators have gone to automation they have become traps utilized by rapists and robbers. A flip of a stop switch can isolate you for a period of

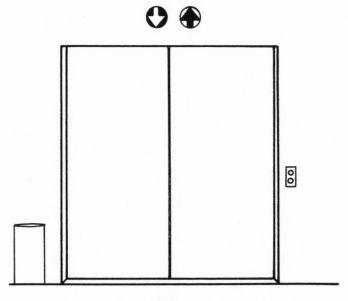

time while an assault takes place. Never get into an elevator with a single stranger or a disreputable looking group. It's better to wait than take a chance. Senior ladies should get off an elevator if she is on it alone and an unknown male enters. Remember - the rapist will attack any female regardless of age.

Learn the emergency procedures recommended for the elevators in your building. In case of trouble, remain calm and follow those procedures. If the elevator stops between floors or the door doesn't open when it is supposed to, keep calm and calm the other passengers. A crowded elevator is no place for panic. As a Senior citizen - take the responsibility of a leader - here's a spot where your age will stand you in good stead.

RESTROOMS

Restrooms - because of their private nature - become attractive places for the rapist and the robber to commit their contemptible acts. This is particularly true in office buildings. They are not heavily populated at any given time except just before or after lunchtime. Most people enter them alone. Restrooms are ordinarily away from other office areas. They are insulated against sound and generally open to anyone. Strict key control should be practiced. Keeping restrooms locked is recommended. (The author is reminded that a rape/murder in an office building with locked restrooms occurred when employees placed tape over the locking mechanism to save the time and notice of obtaining the restroom key and allowed the criminal access.)

All restroom patrons are in a vulnerable position and this is particularly true of Senior Citizens who may be partially disabled. If possible, operate on the buddy system when going to the restroom. Two or more persons reduce the risk from attack by the criminal - a basic coward who prefers to prey on a lone individual.

To repeat - if strict key control is instituted - and no one tries to thwart it - locked restrooms for the workplace is recommended.

HALLWAYS AND CORRIDORS

Most criminal acts in office building occur in other than actual office areas. Vagrants, vandals, and robbers enter most buildings at will. They enter unchallenged to "case out" or study sites for future criminal acts. They lurk in hallways and side corridors ever ready and willing to pounce on unsuspecting workers, they cruise halls seeking unattended work areas or temporarily absent employee desks in order to steal purses, overcoats, attache cases, and other valuables.

Employees should request management to install an entry/exit system to screen individuals. Anyone entering or leaving should be identified as having a legitimate reason for their presence. It may be a bother to show a card or badge several times a day, but it may save your person and your possessions.

Regardless - stay alert and ready to protect yourself and to sound an alarm when entering an empty or sparsely populated working area. Use a whistle, yell "FIRE", and otherwise make a loud commotion if you even suspect an attack. It is far better to suffer a little embarrassment for sounding a false alarm than it is to suffer personal hurt or loss of property. Besides - if the criminal element knows they are in an area of wide awake individuals, they will avoid it.

STORAGE, SUPPLY, AND CONFERENCE ROOMS

Supply rooms and storage rooms are favorite areas for criminals to hide await victims. Rapist or robber, they are aware most workers are alone when they visit these rooms. The criminal may have picked the lock and hidden inside, or they have inserted something in the locking mechanism and entered when no one was around.

If you must go to either of these locations alone, stay alert. If no one is lurking outside the room, check first to see if the door is unlocked. If it is, run to the nearest supervisor and report it. It may have been left unlocked accidentally, but it's always better to be safe than sorry. If the door is locked, open the door carefully, light the interior and look closely before entering. If you see anyone or are attacked, yell "FIRE" and get out of the room if possible. Make it a rule that several of your fellow employees are aware of when you leave for either of these rooms and approximate time you are expected to return.

Conference rooms come in assorted sizes and are seldom monitored. Ordinarily used only when a group is meeting, criminals use them as spots from which to make visual surveys. Have someone with you if you must visit the conference room.

SECURITY PERSONNEL

Many workplaces have in-house or contract agency security guard personnel on duty. They are there for your protection as well as the protection of the physical plant. It is wise to cultivate their friendship and get to know them. They have been trained to react rapidly to all types of emergency situations. They are a permanent part of the american business scene, and if it were not for their services to the community, we would all live in terror.

How many times during a movie or a TV show have you heard the almost automatic cry, "call security" when trouble is at hand?

All security personnel should be present at safety meetings and fire drills with other employees. They should be consulted as to what steps are required in an emergency situation. If an when such a situation occurs, their advice and leadership should be followed to the letter.

FIRE DRILLS

Senior Citizens do not like fire drills - but neither do others. It seems such a waste of time to "play having a fire". However - the properly conducted fire drill - and they should be held often - may save your life in a real fire situation.

Seniors usually move more slowly than others, and they should pay special attention to exit routes and practice all techniques for safety in fire emergencies. The use of elevators in a fire is out and getting down many flights of stairs is a task, but practice anyway. Most lives lost in fires are due to panic, and panic is caused by lack of knowledge as to what to do when fire and smoke appear. You will learn during fire drills the best way in a fire emergency to save yourself is the same as in any other emergency - *REMAIN CALM!*

WHEELCHAIRS AND RAMPS

Modern buildings are required to have ramps for the entry and exit of wheelchair users. Many older buildings do not have them. If they are present, use them with extreme caution. Seniors may not have the strength to propel their vehicles on steep or poorly maintained ramps. If your workplace does not have easily accessible and easy to use ramps, get management to remedy the problem. Until the problem is cured, make arrangements with fellow workers for assistance in entering and leaving the building.

SMOKING AREAS

As we learn more and more about the connection between smoking and lung cancer, the workplace is beginning to remedy its former indifference to the peril. Many shops now designate smoking areas for those who cannot or will not shake the habit. The result has been a marked decline in fires caused by smokers.

If you still work in an area where smoking is permitted, take care to see that all smoking materials are completely extinguished before disposal.

Areas designated for smoking need to have safety rules posted and a check of the area on a constant basis throughout the work day is mandatory. Fire plays no favorites - it hurts everyone.

FIRST AID

A well equipped and up-to-date first aid kit is a must for any workplace. Ask your superior the location of the one assigned to your area. Do a little reading on emergency procedures, and if you have time, take a first aid course and/or cardiopulmonary resuscitation (C.P.R.) course from your local Red Cross center.

Seniors bruise more readily, heal more slowly, and suffer more from falls, as a general rule. They are more subject to heart attacks, strokes, and other general disorders. If a company doctor or nurse is not available in your work area, make sure someone on each shift is familiar with basic first aid principles.

PARKING AREAS

If you use the company parking area, be sure it is well lighted. Light does not prevent crime or criminals from an area, but the fact is - criminals do not like light. An escort service to parking areas after dark is furnished by many companies. If yours doesn't have one - form one. Criminals like to attack loners.

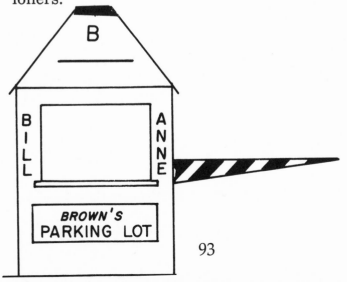

93

INFORMATION YOU SHOULD SHARE

Seniors in the work force should share considerable information with those they ride with, work with, and play with. As we age, we may need a little more time, a little more understanding, and a little more consideration.

If we have arthritis problems, digestive problems, heart problems, or other medical disabilities, we should let our co- workers know about them. Help may be needed at any time, and those who might help need information.

Medical alert bracelets and cards with up-to-date information are valuable - get them if you need them - and notify others of their location on your person. You may not be able to reach for your heart medicine after a sudden seizure, or an allergy may be aggravated by the use of a common antibiotic.

If you have dependents at your home, advise your daily contacts on how to reach them in an emergency.

Be sure your telephone number and address with physical directions on how to get there are on file with your work place phone center. You may need to contact them for help, and they may need to come direct or be able to direct others on how to reach you.

Chapter 5
AT PLAY

Senior Citizens are found in huge number in all segments of the recreational world. We swarm over golf courses, fill swimming pools, populate campgrounds, and compete in trap and skeet events while maintaining an ongoing relationship with fellow hunters. We find ourselves in bowling alleys, on bridal paths, and on handball, racquetball, and tennis courts. We lawn bowl and play major league croquet. We fish from john boats and charter boats.

We cast along lake and creek shores and into the surf.

We are found on cruise ships, in theaters, at baseball parks, and football stadiums, as well as golf and tennis matches. We are highly evident at race tracks (dog and horse), Jai Lai frontons, and auto race ovals.

Senior Citizens participate in, or are spectators to, more recreational events than any group in society. This is probably due to having more leisure time and funds than other groups.

From a security viewpoint, these recreational pursuits have their drawbacks. The criminal mind is aware of our penchant for making the most of our retirement years, and our recreational areas are among their favorite haunts. They realize we are in a more vulnerable position when at play, or as a spectator, and it is to their great advantage.

Pickpockets, purse snatchers, car thieves, and robbers frequent football stadiums, baseball parks, golf and tennis matches - anywhere they find crowds to use as cover as they snatch and run. They delight in rifling cars parked in unprotected areas.

Petty thieves like swimming pool and gymnasium areas. They dress in swim suits and sweat clothes. They mix and mingle with guests. They stand little chance of being discovered.

Parking areas around bowling alleys, Jai Lai frontons, sulky tracks, and other after dark operations afford criminals many opportunities. The robber, the rapist, and the burglar work the lots, stealing automobiles, stealing from automobiles, and assaulting their victims with small chance of being recognized or discovered.

In general, ladies should keep both hands ready to grasp their purse when in crowds, carrying the purse close to the body. Men should carry their wallets securely anchored in a position difficult to reach by another. Returning to the automobile or other transportation after dark should be done with caution. A flashlight makes a good defensive weapon in case of attack, used as a beam into the eyes to blind the assailant and as a club used as a fencer uses a foil - jabbing into any area possible. It is always best to look under the auto and into the interior before entering.

Joggers and walkers should stay on well lighted and heavily used paths. Rapists and strong arm robbers readily assault Seniors without apparent defenses. If you are a jogger or walker - or even a stroller - wear a whistle around your neck. A shrill whistle may drive off an attacker fearing detection. Screaming "FIRE" as you move the whistle to your lips can help. And - since injuries or other physical problems occur frequently to Seniors doing strenuous exercises - it is easier to get enough lung power to blast an alarm on a whistle than it is to use your voice. Night joggers and walkers must remember to wear light colored clothing, preferably with reflective material included. Carrying a flashlight after dark is always a good security measure.

FISHING

Senior Citizens should never go fishing alone in a boat. Each year, a great number of Seniors lose their lives after falling from boats, being swamped, or having their boat upset. Most mishaps can be avoided, the best way being to have a companion. Two heads and other faculties are better than one, especially in boating.

Boating security and safety measures include wearing, at all times around the water, proper floatation articles such as life vests and boat cushions. Having the vessel properly equipped with running lights, fire extinguishers, anchors, and mooring lines is a legal requirement. Care in handling fuel supplies, having extra paddles or oars, and a supply of flares is recommended.

A simple first aid kit should be a part of your fishing gear. Hooks, fish fins, and knives puncture the skin. Insect bites and skinned knuckles from repairing engines and fighting big fish are common. Insect repellent and a sterilizing solution such as wood alcohol or hydrogen peroxide can be most welcome.

Alcohol and water sports do not mix any better than alcohol and gasoline. Fishing and boating people are subject to being soaked, sometimes in very cold water, and alcohol aggravates hypothermia. Clear heads make for better navigation and fishing - wait until your catch has been cleaned before that tall cool one or hot toddy is used in a toast.

POOLS AND SPAS

Enjoyable they are, but swimming pools and spas are the source of far too many injuries to Seniors. Entering the cooling waters of the pool or the warming swirls of the spa tends to make us relax into almost utter carelessness - if they are on the home property, the feeling is magnified, and danger is often overlooked.

No one should ever swim alone. Cramps, dizziness, and fainting in water can be deadly. If you must swim alone, always stay next to the edge of the pool. If something goes wrong you may be able to get out of the water before it's to late.

Every pool should be properly lighted and have several ring buoys with strong lines attached. A long pole with hook to offer a struggling swimmer can be a life saver.

All electrical pool equipment should be checked annually and no electrical appliance of any kind should be put in use without a ground fault circuit interrupter.

Pool decks must be kept free of buoys, chairs, and debris. Slick spots should be cleaned and made skid-proof.

Drinking in the pool is an "invitation to trouble" and remaining in a pool while it is raining or a storm is in progress is an invitation to disaster.

Every pool should have a first aid kit in full view of swimmers and spectators. The kit should contain the names and locations of the nearest emergency treatment centers with telephone numbers and instructions on how to reach them. The list should contain the names of doctors, fire houses, rescue units, ambulance centers, hospitals, and the police.

Spa areas should contain the information given for pools plus a note that spa water temperatures must be checked each time entry is made. Do not use a spa if you have been drinking alcoholic beverages. If you are taking medication or suffer from heart disease, diabetes, or fluctuating blood pressure, do not use the spa without prior medical approval.

Pools and spas are considered in legal circles as "attractive nuisances", bringing unwanted trespassers who have the right to sue you for damages in case they are injured. Protect yourself by fencing your pool, locking your spa, posting No Trespassing signs, and forbidding use without your immediate presence.

BOATING

One of the unexplained mysteries of life is why an individual will spend five or more decades taking care of life and limbs and then, a week after retirement, buy a boat with a giant sized engine and take off in unfamiliar waters with little more knowledge than how to get the rig started and underway.

Overloaded boats, boating while drinking, lack of life preservers, striking obstacles in unknown waters, running out of fuel, having engine problems, and getting lost are among the reasons many Seniors suffer serious injury or loss of life in marine recreation.

Senior Citizens with little experience in boating should take the time to become thoroughly familiar with their equipment. Learn what it can do - and what it cannot do. All waters - oceans, gulfs, lakes, rivers, and canals are unforgiving of carelessness and foolhardiness.

Wherever you purchase your boating equipment, have the sales force instruct you in operation of it, in detail, or direct you to someone who can. Contact the nearest power squadron of the U.S. Coast Guard Auxiliary. Take their basic course in navigation and water safety. It is inexpensive; it is thorough and may save your life. It will turn each of your ventures afloat into times of pleasure.

It is recommended you take an experienced boater with you on your maiden voyage and until you have learned the practical side of boating. Make sure you have properly licensed and lighted your boat and trailer, and that all safety items have been installed. This will protect you and others on all navigable waters.

Weather stations give small boaters information during their daily forecasts, and although we know how often the weather info is wrong - heed them. When they post storm warnings, stay in port. Wind and water joined can become a formidable foe.

Fresh and salt water marinas are available in

most areas. Owned by municipalities or private entities, they can help solve boating problems. If you do not use a marina for boat storage, take care where you store it. The theft of boats and motors is a major criminal enterprise costing owners millions of dollars each year.

Boats left in back or side yards, under carports, and otherwise poorly secured are prime targets of thieves. Boats and motors are easily sold, and the thieves are difficult to catch.

If your boat is normally left on a trailer, lock the boat to the trailer and the motor to the boat. Then, lock the trailer so it is difficult to move. Storing your boat out of sight is recommended. Other boating gear, including fishing tackle, should be locked up separately.

Marine equipment thieves seldom run the risk of being discovered with their loot. They sell it for whatever they can get and seek out other careless owners for victims. If you suffer a loss, notify the police, wildlife officers, and marine patrols immediately. You have (we hope) etched your ID number (drivers' license) onto several parts of your boat and motor and have serial numbers for each along with registration papers. If you have taken pictures of the rig, it will help to locate and identify it.

HIKING

Senior Citizens are found on trails in almost every part of the world. It seems to be a favorite

pastime. Security rules for hikers are the same as for other outdoors oriented persons such as bird watchers, nature photographers, and stargazers.

Senior Citizens should fit themselves with proper shoes for outdoor activities. Shoes made of leather, light in weight, with solid non-slip soles, and six to eight inches high will protect ankles. Waterproofing should be built in or applied before hiking. A half size over your regular shoe size is recommended since feet swell after long walks (and with age). In addition, the extra half size allows for natural cotton or woolen socks that help absorb moisture and cushion the foot. Break them in with short walks before going on a long hike. Senior Citizens feet are not immune to blisters and bunions!

Hiking clothes should be of natural fibers and worn in layers. Silk, cotton, and wool help keep the body cool and help keep it warm. Wearing clothes in layers makes it easier to shed top garments during the day when temperatures rise. Layering also helps prevent hypothermia which can occur during sudden rainstorms, windstorms, or from a tumble or wading into a body of water.

Hats are musts for hikers. They protect the head (you lose more heat through the head than any other part of the body), and if you wisely choose a broad brimmed hat, you have added protection from the sun and rain.

A small but accurate compass is desirable for all hikers. Experienced hikers know how to make mental notes about natural landmarks using rock formations, fallen trees, and variations in waterways as they hike. However - anyone can get lost. The compass will help you find your way out of your situation as long as you remain calm and **DO NOT PANIC**. It is recommended hikers carry a whistle and a reflective metal mirror to signal others when they are lost. The human body can exist three days without water and up to three weeks without food.

A small but well packed first aid kit should be in every hikers pack. Band-aids, gauze, lip balm, a disinfectant, and insect repellent should be included. A sunscreen rated above 15 with paba or equivalent applied an hour before going into sunlight can help prevent sunburn and possible skin cancer.

Hikers should carry a small butane burning lighter. They are better than matches because moisture doesn't hurt them. They have a long flame that reaches the temperature it takes to ignite wood, and wind doesn't blow out the flame.

While we were growing into our present senior status, astronauts began wearing spacesuits made from mylar. Blankets made from the material are available - a small 4' X 6' keeps a person warm. Light in weight and costing little, they fold into a small space, capture body heat, and are waterproof. These blankets can double as a poncho or a small tent and have been used as temporary water containers. Do not go hiking without one.

Criminals are not as liable to be in wide open spaces as they are in crowded areas, but it pays to keep your eyes open. Rapists and small time robbers sometimes work places where hikers congregate. Rules for streets and sidewalks apply to hikers, especially those who use well marked trails.

SWIMMING

Safety and security rules for swimmers at home also apply to those who swim in lakes and rivers or at ocean and gulf beaches. However, added rules are in order for ocean and sea swimmers, and some limitations are placed on swimmers in lakes and rivers. Gulf and ocean beaches have changing currents and undertow is of concern. Drop-offs and obstructions may be found in lakes and rivers along with broken bottles and cans thoughtless people toss into our waters. Water depths vary, and divers should test unknown waters before diving into them.

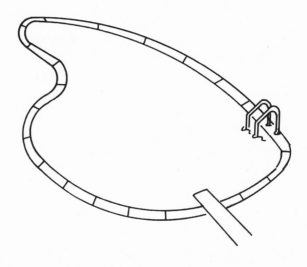

Natural bodies of water sometimes play host to snakes and alligators as well as leeches and insects, but the greatest concern of swimmers in these waters is man-made pollution from runoff waters and sewerage.

The pool swimmers first rule - ***Do Not Swim Alone*** - applies everywhere. If you swim at supervised areas, obey the lifeguard on duty. Pay attention to signal flags and water conditions. If he/she orders you out of the water, get out at once. There is an excellent reason for the request.

If you get caught in an outgoing tide due to undertow or any other reason - **DO NOT PANIC!** Float with the tide until help arrives or you are able to find a spot where the water is shallow enough to stand. If you get caught in a river or stream current, swim with the current and angle toward the shore until you are safe. To repeat - **DO NOT PANIC!**

Almost every incident of drowning stems from a person losing their composure.

CAMPING

Some forms of camping, like other activities, are safer than others. The recreational vehicle or camper pulling into a managed area is more secure than the camper pitching a tent in a wilderness area. Criminals, cowards at heart, prefer to attack the loner. Crime in camping spots is not as widespread as it is in other areas. The author has pitched camp in many diverse locations and has never experienced a loss or known of any loss taking place in any campsite where he camped. However, it pays to take precautions. (In one camp some years ago, a pair of elderly ladies camped in a pickup truck with a topper. Each night when they retired, they placed a pair of large sized muddy boots on the steps leading into their sleeping quarters. In the morning when they emerged, they smiled and put the boots back into the topper.)

When entering a camping area with management at hand, ask what kind of security is offered, expected response time, nearest telephone, and how to quickly reach assistance.

When selecting your campsite, ask about potentials for flash floods, forest fires, and evacuation routes. If going into wilderness area, obtain the same information. Select a site with as secure a location as is possible.

Do not become a source of fire. Take

precautions with open flames and equipment that might lead to fire. Study your camp area and make a mental note of exit points available in case of a disaster. Like boy scouts, "be prepared".

HUNTING

Criminals seldom take on hunters. The reason being is the hunter carries protection in the form of firearms or bows and arrows.

However - the general rules of security set forth for fishing and hiking activities are the same for hunters.

Hunters face another reason for special caution since they carry and use a variety of weapons. If you are not an experienced hunter, take your hunting weapon to a training center and practice with it under the eye of an experienced instructor. If you are experienced and obtain a new hunting item, try it before you head for the hunt.

Keeping weapons loaded while away from the hunt is not safe. Guns should be unloaded on the way to and the way back from a hunting trip. If you have weapons at home, make sure they are unloaded, that ammunition is away from unauthorized hands, and your firearms are away from children. Trigger guards should be on every gun, except when the gun is in use.

While hunting, wear distinctive clothing. Never shoot at anything until you *know* what it is. Keep your fellow hunters informed as to your location. Carrying a compass, butane lighter, a whistle, and a reflective mirror is most prudent.

Hunters should carry additional items in their first aid kits. Extra bandaging material, materials to improvise a stretcher, and a recommended tourniquet are among them. Accidents are caused on hunting trips as elsewhere. Hunters bagging big game specimens chance injury in removing carcasses. Back injuries and hernias often can be traced to a successful hunt.

RV'S

Follow the recommended maintenance schedule your mechanic provides for your recreational vehicle each time you take it out and each time you return with it. Basic precautions are to fuel it properly, keep all belts and hoses in good condition, know the oil level is okay, and that tires have good treads. A large, well supplied tool kit for emergency repairs is recommended.

Thieves steal RV's when given the opportunity. Installing a warning signal to sound if the vehicle is moved illegally, cutting off valves to fuel supplies, and installing an ignition cutoff are some methods to be used in theft prevention.

When you are away from your RV, keep it locked. It may prevent pilferage, vandalism, and perhaps theft. Have serial numbers from the engine and chassis of your RV where they can be easily found and engrave your ID number (drivers' license) on items in the vehicle. Thieves show some reluctance to stealing inscribed articles, and many pawn brokers will not accept them.

TENTS

Modern tents made of flame resistant materials, but it is wise to keep open flame away from them. Gasoline, propane, or alcohol fueled stoves and lights should not be kept in tents. To supply light in the interior, flashlights and other battery powered lights are preferable.

Do not build an open fire near a tent. Sparks may damage the tent. A tent does not make a barrier effective against humans or large animals such as bears and the bigger cats. When you use a tent, keep these facts in mind.

GOLF COURSES

Golf courses are frequently the target of the criminal element. When we take to the golf course, we are relatively unprotected. Pro shops and clubhouses contain easily disposed of equipment and cash receipts.

If you are a member at a course, discuss the establishment of a security system with members of the greens committee. Private and public courses should see to it their superintendents, professionals, and other supervisory personnel have basic security training. All golf course personnel should have first aid and CPR training.

When you pay your greens fee at a strange golf course, ask what type of security is afforded. Public courses are more vulnerable to criminal activity than private courses. The criminal golfer is alike in appearance to other golfers. It is easy for a thief, dressed as a golfer, to mingle with other golfers, to meander out to unloading zones and spot items to steal. Golf items are easy to sell. It takes only a few moments to inscribe your ID number on your golf clubs, cart, and other items for identification.

While on the course, report any suspicious looking or acting persons to the course ranger. Vandals and souvenir collectors plague courses uprooting markers, stealing flags, and defacing signs. Women golfers are susceptible to the rapist, especially late in the day and should keep a sharp lookout. A golf club makes a good weapon.

Thieves hang around locker rooms to pilfer from lockers and rob patrons. Lock your locker each time you leave it. If you have large sums of money or expensive jewelry, take them to the pro shop and have them put in a safe.

If you visit the 19th hole - partake with moderation - especially if you are driving. And - when you leave for the parking lot, keep your eyes and ears open. Having your key ready to open the door instantly is a sound security measure. Your car key, held firmly between thumb and forefinger, is an effective jabbing weapon if you come under attack. Long key keeper bars, similar to the NASP Key Keeper of the National Association of Security Personnel also makes a handy repellant.

TENNIS COURTS

Tennis players suffer losses by carrying wallets and purses into the court area and leaving them unattended. Better to lock them in the trunk of your car.

Lighted tennis courts are popular, particularly with people who work during the day. Players using night facilities should follow the security methods advised for other night parking lots.

Tennis players have one advantage - they carry rackets which make excellent protective weapons.

PICNICS AND COOKOUTS

Hospital emergency rooms report crowded emergency rooms on weekends and holidays can often be traced to senior chefs exhibiting their skills at cooking, but failing to follow safety rules.

Seniors suffering injuries have usually been careless. Using charcoal in unventilated areas, cooking barefooted, handling hot utensils without protective gloves, using gasoline or kerosene lighter fluid on open flames are among oft quoted reasons for these "accidents".

Before you take over the grill, heed the following suggestions.

1. Use only waterproofed UL approved cords, light sockets, and plugs outside.

2. Use non-glare lights to outline steps and other yard items.

3. Never use charcoal inside. Take extreme care of fire on windy days.

4. Keep a bucket of water and a fire extinguisher near your cooking area.

5. Use insulated heat resistant gloves and long handled tools.

6. Use waterproof and non-glare lights after dark.

7. Never use gasoline or kerosene to start your fire.

When you picnic, look over the picnic spot before unloading supplies. If the area looks unsafe, or unsavory characters seem to be present, avoid the spot.

SPECTATOR LOCATIONS

Senior Citizens attending events which draw large crowds are more vulnerable than other citizens. Their agility, voices, and overall strength may be reduced by medications and the aging process. They are favored targets of criminals who specialize in working such events. Senior Citizens suffer more from heat, cold, snow, and rain. They are more apt to have problems while climbing up and down steps and from jostling by the crowd. Medical conditions are often aggravated by exposure and excitement. Spectators at many events become unruly and violent. Seniors may, for reasons outlined above, find it difficult to get out of the way.

SECURITY FOR SENIOR CITIZENS

Senior Citizens attending large crowd events should carry as small amount of cash as possible, leaving wallets and purses in the trunk of their car. Pickpockets and purse snatchers use crowds to cover their escape.

When parking at stadiums and other arenas, roll windows all the way to the top and make sure all doors are locked. Do not leave valuable items on seats or dashboards where they can be seen. Put these items in the trunk while stowing your wallet and purse. Your car dealer can install an extra secure trunk lock economically. If you leave your car parked in remote areas, this lock can save valuables. Installation will cost less than the damage suffered from a one time prying open of the trunk lid.

If necessary to carry wallets and/or purses, men should guard wallets with a chain or inside shirt (not coat) pocket and ladies should clutch the purse close to the body. Over the shoulder purse straps are often used to pull the victim to the side or to the ground if the purse is swinging freely. Seniors should not hurry up or down steps. Becoming exhausted increases vulnerability and falls become more serious as time goes by.

Chapter 6

STREETS, SIDEWALKS, AND BUILDINGS

Most of us, now in our golden years, grew up in places where street crime was almost non-existent. We had no fear walking the streets and sidewalks of our community at any time of the day or night. We did not hesitate to look for a friend or an address in another town or city, believing the strangers we would meet would help us as we helped others in our hometown. However - that feeling of security has gone the way of the "handshake" contract, stopping to help a stranded motorist, or picking up a hitchhiker.

Street crimes vary in type and severity, robbery and rape being the most common. Many can be avoided by *always following security rules*. These rules must be followed each time we leave our home, our friends homes, our hotel or motel, stores, businesses, or other islands of safety.

Anytime you go walking, jogging, strolling, or shopping, take someone with you. Criminals prefer to attack loners.

Try to complete your chores away from home before dark. The less exposure, the less chance of becoming a victim.

If you must be away from home after dark, and must return after dark, carry a flashlight. A flashlight beam aimed into the eyes of an attacker while you yell "FIRE" at the top of your voice may frighten off an assailant. The flashlight is a handy weapon when used as a punching tool at the face or stomach of an attacker.

Get a good metal whistle and carry it when you venture into darkness. It is easier to blow a whistle than to yell, and the blast may bring help and frighten the coward who does not want to be seen and identified.

If your keys are attached to a key keeping bar along the lines of the one used by members of the

National Association of Security Personnel, you have a defensive weapon that can be used in several ways. Carrying it with keys dangling, it makes noise without revealing what is being carried. When carried with keys dangling, it is easy to swing the keys straight up through the groin area of your confronter. At the top of the swing, it is in a position so the keys can be brought downward across the face. Swinging and yelling "FIRE" may bring help and save your life and property. If you carry your keys on a conventional ring or holder, place a key between thumb and forefinger, and you have a jabbing weapon to help ward off attackers.

If these actions sound harsh - they are - and should be. Anyone who attacks you deserves any damage you may be able to inflict.

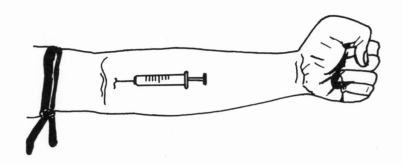

WALKING AND JOGGING

The popularity of walking and jogging has prompted rapists and robbers to be on the lookout for participants. Follow the suggestions given in the chapter titled "At Play" and never let your guard down. Having a companion when on streets or sidewalks is an excellent method of avoiding trouble.

DAYS AND NIGHTS

The professional criminal, and there are far too many of them, prefers to work under cover of darkness, but as the drug problem increases, there is a trend toward more daylight crime. Another reason for less after dark crime is because citizens are spending more time at home after dark, and the criminal has fewer choices. The continuing demise of the movie house, the theatre, and after dark entertainment keeps most of us home watching television and off the streets.

The use of "crack" - the cheaper kin of cocaine - has resulted in a more crazed user, ready to attack at any time. Avoid anyone who appears to be drunk or otherwise physically impaired. They are dangerous individuals and will do anything to feed their habits.

MALLS

The shopping mall now has most of the stores, most of the shoppers - and unfortunately - most of the criminal element.

Senior Citizens populate malls in great numbers. They are favorite targets of robbers, rapists, pickpockets, and purse snatchers.

Shopping with someone is good security. Holding the purse close to the body and keeping the wallet in an inside short pocket is advised. Never enter the restroom area of a mall alone. If no one is available, ask mall management to have security personnel escort you. Seniors in restrooms are very vulnerable.

When parking at a mall, park as close to the entrance as possible and get in the habit of parking under a light. If parking on a slope, turn the wheels of your auto against the curb to prevent it from rolling. It will also make it more difficult to tow away or load onto a carrier.

Returning to your vehicle from the mall, keep your eyes on loiterers or others in the vicinity. If your car has strange people around it, return to the mall, and ask security personnel for assistance. After dark, it is advisable to shine the beam of your flashlight under the car and into the interior. Criminals like to hide under cars and enter them, if possible.

STORES

While shopping in individual shops, approach checkout stations with caution and remain vigilant until your bill has been paid. Try not to carry large amounts of cash, but if you have large amounts, do not flash it. Keep credit cards and ID materials away from your cash. Do not place your purse or wallet on the counter or take your hands off it. There are many thieves hanging around waiting for your careless moment.

If you see someone shoplifting - notify store

security personnel or the nearest clerk. Shoplifters are criminals, and the cost of merchandise they steal is passed on to you in the form of higher prices. It is also in your best interest to stop shoplifters since a struggle with them may lead to violence and inadvertently involve you.

If you are in a store that is being robbed, keep a low profile. Do as the robber says and use every bit of observative powers and memory you possess. You may be able to identify the robber later. Note the clothing worn, the shape of the head, color of hair and eyes, any marks such as tatoos or scars, and general body build. Height and weight estimates and any pronounced individual trait such as a limp, lisp, or voice sound may help put the criminal behind bars where he or she belongs.

LIBRARIES, MUSEUMS, AND ATTRACTIONS

Libraries are safe enough places most of the time, but they become a magnet attracting rapists and robbers after dark. The rules suggested for leaving any building apply in this situation. Senior Citizens are frequent users of libraries, and after browsing and perhaps checking out books or records, the mind is far from thoughts of crime. The criminal knows this and will take advantage if we drop our guard for a moment.

Museums are not heavily populated on a steady basis with the exception of a few like the Smithsonian. Seniors are usually those who frequent them, and criminals are aware of it. Taking advantage of low density crowds and knowing the senior usually has a few extra dollars makes the museum visitor an enticing target for the robber, pickpocket, and purse snatcher. Fortunately, attacks within museum building are not common, but care must be taken as we approach and leave them.

Attractions are invitations to pickpockets, purse snatchers, robbers, and car thieves. The pickpocket and purse snatcher depend on crowds to shield their escape. By keeping close tabs on wallets and purses, we can prevent many losses. Robbers take advantage of the happy mood of people who have been viewing and enjoying attractions. They lie in wait to rob and molest!

Do not hesitate to go to security personnel working at the attraction with any request pertaining to your security. They are anxious to see that you have a pleasant visit to their place of employment.

BANKS, S & L's, AND INVESTMENT HOUSES

When Willie Sutton was asked why he robbed banks, he replied, "That's where the money is." He was right then and would be right today - and criminals are well aware of it.

Senior Citizens use banks and savings and loans more often than any segment of our society. They use direct deposit of pension and social security checks, make and receive mortgage payments, and use many other facilities of these institutions.

Drive-in facilities used at most banks and savings and loans have reduced the number of robberies at or near the building proper, but the use of automatic teller machines has offset these gains.

The drive-up is a time saving addition but multiple lanes place many of us at high risk. It is difficult for tellers to see more than one or two lanes and petty thieves lie in wait to snatch conveyor tubes from unwary depositers. When you approach the drive-in post, have all windows and doors locked. Roll down the window next to the teller post - reach and get the tube - bring it into the vehicle. Roll the window up before loading the tube with your transaction, then roll it down and place tube in the sending unit. Keep your eye on the teller and as soon as your tube starts back, be ready to retrieve it and bring it inside the car to check for accuracy.

When approaching an automatic teller machine, look carefully. If there are others around, wait until they have completed their business before moving in. Keep your eyes moving and return to your vehicle if trouble is apparent. Robbers, particularly those with drug habits, hang around ATM's awaiting unwary customers.

ROBBERY

The first rule regarding robbery is that money and material things can be replaced - your life cannot.

Robbery taking place on streets is a very touchy situation. Robbers are chancing easy arrest and are generally more nervous than when robbing someone in a home or business setting where walls afford privacy for their crime.

If you are surprised by a robber, authorities say your best defense is to comply with demands for money and valuables. Offer resistance only if physical harm appears likely. You are better off remaining as calm as possible under the circumstances. Make an effort to note everything you can about your assailant. Clothing worn, sound of the voice, height, weight, general build, color of hair, identifying marks, and any unusual feature should be committed to memory.

If you must resist, scream "FIRE", kick at the

groin area, and run. As soon as you find help, jot down or tell someone everything that happened as you remember it. If there was another witness to the robbery, ask them to give a description of the robber and to relate every detail they remember. Make a full report to law enforcement personnel at the first opportunity.

If you are assaulted, in any manner, get medical help quickly. This is tremendously important in the case of rape and attempted rape. Many criminals are carriers of the AIDS virus due to their lifestyle as drug users, homosexuals, or bisexuals. Do not clean up before getting to a medical facility since blood and semen samples are needed for testing. Recent advances in identifying DNA prints from blood and semen samples is leading to increased convictions of assaulting criminals.

DEMEANOR

Since the criminal is basically a coward, their favored prey is one who appears frightened and unsure of themselves. They operate like predators in the wild, waiting for a loner, or for one showing signs of disability. The best defense when you and/or your companions venture out in sparsely populated areas is to walk confidently, keeping eyes open observing others passing you - in either direction. Knowing where you are going and how you are going to get there is practicing good security.

If you suspect someone is following you - stop

and look directly at them - if your suspicions are correct, and you are being followed - move alertly into any area where there are other people.

WEATHER INFLUENCES

Unusual or severe weather conditions are often used by criminals to hide their activities on streets, sidewalks, and in stores.

During rainstorms, they use the umbrella as a weapon, depend upon people to be careless in locking their autos, and use weather sounds to muffle victims cries for help. They move into shelters where close contact aids them in picking pockets and snatching purses. If they are detected, they flee into the storm.

FATIGUE

Seniors tire more easily and require more frequent rest stops. Plan your walks to take advantage of the shortest and safest path. Know where you are headed and how you plan to get there and return. When you stop to rest, survey the resting area closely - if suspicious characters are around, keep moving.

INTERSECTION

When approaching intersections watch for crossing traffic and potential attempts to block your path. Taking advantage of the slowing necessary at street junctions, assailants may try to open your auto door and either pull you out or get in with you.

Another criminal trick is for the car in front of you at an intersection to remain motionless while a confederate closes in on you from the rear so you cannot escape - another reason for you to refrain from driving to close to or "tailgating" another.

STREET LIGHTS

Since the criminal element does not like light, street lights can be friendly havens. Whenever possible, park your auto under or near a streetlight. When walking, try to stay in the glow of these lights, and if you are being followed, get into the full light as quickly as possible. One planned to be a victim, standing in light yelling "FIRE" is not an inviting target.

SHRUBBERY

When walking, stay near the middle of the sidewalk or street. Shrubbery offers hiding places for would be assailants - so do trees. Parking your auto in the shade of a tree is nice but check closely when parking and returning to your car. Make certain the tree doesn't shelter one who would do you harm.

" HEAD 'EM UP – MOVE 'EM OUT"

Chapter 7

MOVING

Some 35 million Americans, a great number of them Senior Citizens, move each year. Across town, to a different city, to another state, or to a foreign country, the task has become a complicated process with great security risks.

The day we called upon a neighbor or relative to help load and unload household and other goods has disappeared. Today, we hire out the entire operation to a professional, rent a truck and do it ourselves, or combine the two. In either situation, we must not let our guard down.

You - and your goods - are highly vulnerable during a move. Your mind is on a number of things you must do. Your furniture is in your hands or those of another. You may have children, Seniors, or pets with you - perhaps a combination - and the last thing that crosses your mind is the thought of danger.

The criminal eyes your moving as a golden opportunity. Other dangers present themselves during the journey.

To lessen the dangers inherent in any move, it is wise to make an overall plan. Careful planning with attention to safety and security will make your move more pleasant and perhaps save you and your possessions from disaster.

First on the list should be confirmation of your move with present and future landlords and other agents concerned. Set a definite time for departure and near as possible arrival at the other end. Do not discuss these times with anyone other than those who need to know.

The author has always been against the practice of placing "For Sale" or "For Rent" signs at a residence, either "By Owner" or by real estate companies. They are advertisements of unprotected property and may cause many problems. The criminal, the vandal, and others have a perfect excuse for "casing out" the property in the guise of

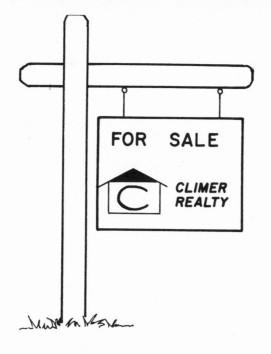

a prospective buyer or rentor. Neighbors tend to ignore strangers when these signs appear.

Security should also be on your mind when you have prospective buyers looking at your house. Thieves and burglars use open houses and other real estate viewings to spot items to steal and to make notes of access points. Do not let anyone go through your home alone and make sure the real estate agent understands that prospects are to be accompanied at all times and closely observed. Explaining the working of security systems in place prior to having a signed contract is asking for trouble.

Holding a yard sale before moving is a common practice and one used by criminals to solicit information as to times and dates of moves. The same applies to buyers of second-hand furniture. It is okay to have these sales, but the time you plan on leaving is of no concern to customers.

There are many items to consider when making your moving plan. You may not need all of the following suggestions. You may wish to add more, but the idea is to plan as safe and secure a move as is possible.

WHAT TO MOVE

Moving brings hard decisions as to what items to move and what should be sold or given away. Make a list and stick to it. Consider the size of the house you are leaving and the size of the one you are moving into. If you are moving from a cold climate to a warm climate, sell items such as snow chains, snow shoes, galoshes, and rubber boots. Make travel arrangements for pets or find them a good home. Return any borrowed items you have and collect those you have loaned out. If you are moving lawn equipment, drain the fuel and oil. If you are moving a boat or pull type camper, re-pack trailer wheel bearings and make sure tires will make the trip safely. On a long move, an extra wheel or tire becomes a necessity.

CANCELLATIONS, ETC.

Cancel newspapers and other routine home delivery services several days prior to actual departure. If you know your new mailing address, tell your bank, savings and loan, stock broker, and others. Give them an effective date but make it a few days later than your expected arrival. Notify the post office of the date you wish them to begin forwarding mail and have them start several days before you leave. Numerous instances of criminals being tipped off to moves from postal employees have been recorded in recent years.

Close out your safe deposit box, arrange transfer letters from civic, church, and fraternal groups. Be sure your insurance agent has adequately covered you and your goods for the trip.

The day before you leave, notify law enforcement personnel of your estimated time of departure and how you might be reached in case of an emergency. Let them know who will be in charge of your house. Then, notify utility companies you are leaving.

The day you leave, make a final check of closets and storage, pick up yard items you haven't already packed, prop open the doors of refrigerator and freezer, and double check to be sure all windows and doors are locked. Turn off water at the meter, do the same for gas service, and *pull the electric master switch* before giving up your keys.

ON THE ROAD

With an up-to-date road map you marked during your planning sessions and in recently serviced vehicles, you are ready to go. A good flashlight, emergency flares, can of compressed air for tires, and an extra set of auto keys should be with you in addition to other items covered in a previous chapter. Paper towels and a chest with refreshments will come in handy. An ample supply of any needed prescription medicines is a must. A packet with copies of important papers in the glove compartment may be useful. Originals should have been forwarded to yourself at your new location, certified, with signature demanded by addressee only.

HIGHWAY SECURITY

Modern highways are far from being safe. Precautions can make a difference and should be kept in mind. Driving with doors locked and windows at least three quarters of the way up is recommended. Stop every two hours and take a stretch break. Senior Citizens' muscles and sinews need limbering up from time to time, and getting the blood circulating after sitting for long periods makes you a safer driver.

Whenever you stop, especially on open stretches of the road, look before you step out of your vehicle. Snakes, oil slicks, nails, broken glass, and other debris can cause trouble.

When pulling into a rest stop, look it over before turning off your engine. Many stops are unattended and are selected by criminals and drifters as spots from which to prey on traveling people. If the area looks suspicious, move on. The more people you see in rest areas, the less likely trouble will arise. Restrooms are the most dangerous place at rest stops so enter them carefully.

If you are travelling with a moving van, or driving it yourself, make sure proper locks have been installed and are being used during the trip. Always remove keys from any vehicle when you leave the driver's seat - no matter how short your stay may be. Park your van, or have it parked, so it is easy to move away from the parking area. If you are on the road overnight, park your car and/or moving vehicle under a streetlight. Notify your lodging manager of the location.

Take care when approaching detour signs. Note carefully the number and quality. Sometimes, criminals use detour signs as a ruse to get motorists off the road.

If another vehicle seems to be following you, pull in at the next populated stop and observe. Cowardly criminals will often give up the chase if they know their quarry is suspicious.

UPON ARRIVAL

If you have been on a "do it yourself" move, your time of arrival at the new house is not as important as if you had someone do it for you. In the latter case, you should arrive before or at the same time as the mover. You can then check to see if everything loaded is unloaded, and if damage has been sustained, you can file an immediate claim. Allowing a mover to have a key to a house is unwise for many reasons, and you can enumerate them yourself.

It is recommended you have the following items readily available when you roll into your new driveway:

1. Comfortable clothing.
2. Light bulbs in various sizes.
3. Garbage bags.
4. Paper towels.
5. Electrical extension cords.

You may have to eat your first meal picnic style, and it helps to have paper plates, plastic cups, and table settings. A roll of foil, a roll of wax paper, a can opener, and perhaps a pot or pan with a bar of soap and a few sponges may come in handy.

AT YOUR NEW PLACE

The overall plan you made prior to your move is ready for more study now that you have completed your trip.

While furniture and boxes are being unloaded, check fuse boxes or circuit breaker boxes if power has been turned on and the master switch has been pulled. Check faucets, toilets, and other plumbing before turning on water at the meter. If these utilities have not been turned on, make sure listed items are checked when the electrician and plumber arrive. Most utility companies and plumbing companies will not turn on power and water unless someone is present. A box sitting on a burner someone forgot to turn off has caused many fires in unsupervised hook- ups.

After power, water, and gas have been supplied, test pilot lights, water heaters, air conditioning units. All wall receptacles and other outlets should be checked so you know they work properly and safely. If your telephone has been installed, check all phone jacks.

CHECKING MOVED ITEMS

Whether you moved yourself, had assistance in moving, or contracted the entire job, you should check all items. This is very important if you hired any of the moving and should be done as soon as possible.

Missing or damaged goods claims need to be filed promptly, and it is best to check before anyone responsible, other than yourself, departs your new home. Whether the claim is against the mover or an insurance company, detailed listing is required.

SECURITY CHECK

Unless you are moving into a new house, you should have all locks changed or re-keyed. You do not know how many keys have been made for locks by previous occupants. If the house was on the market, you know keys were loaned for inspection by would be buyers. Many shrewd thieves make it a habit to ask for late afternoon or early morning inspections so they can have keys made while oweners or agents are absent.

Check all windows for signs of previous entry and make sure any sliding glass doors have the track block as well as locking extras.

The steps to take to make your new house more secure are the same that are recommended to be taken in the chapter "Home Sweet Home".

AND FINALLY

Make it a point to meet some of your new neighbors. You may need them at a future date - and they may need a good neighbor.

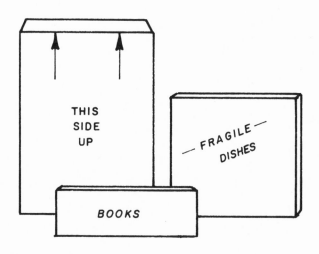

PASSPORT

UNITED STATES
of AMERICA

MARTHA

Chapter 8
TRAVEL

Senior Citizens are world travelers. They visit every spot on the globe they are allowed to visit. They travel on foot, on bicycles, on motorcycles, in automobiles, in vans, in recreational vehicles, aboard trains, on ocean liners, aboard tramp steamers, and in the air on large and small airplanes.

In publications catering to the interests of Senior Citizens, reader responses show 80% of the respondents list travel as their favorite activity.

SECURITY FOR SENIOR CITIZENS

Seniors travel for a variety of reasons. Some realizing a lifelong ambition to visit certain locations - some retracing steps taken during a global war - some because they like to find new experiences and meet new people. Whatever the reasons - Senior Citizens are on the go!!!

Travel - domestic and foreign - is not as safe as we would like it to be. Terrorist regimes in many countries give concern. People in many areas, care not for human life. During recent years, we have seen many hijackings of planes, the taking of numerous hostages, and many senseless bombings. We never know if our traveling companions will be bombers or assassins. However, we cannot let such possibilities deter us from going wherever we choose. By using caution and common sense, we need have no fear, but we must be constantly alert and "think security".

Travel terminals have stiffened security measures in recent years, particularly airports. They sometimes may be over zealous in their work but always obey their rules and regulations. If you are about to travel on public transportation and you detect suspicious looking individuals, ask security to keep an eye on them.

When entering an airport, be alert and carefully scan the area you are entering. Pickpockets and purse snatchers like to work crowds at airports. They know the traveler is looking forward to a trip coming up or is happy to be returning home. They know either frame of mind

**PUT
THEM IN
A
SAFE**

makes for carelessness. Never carry large sums of cash. Travelers' checks can be replaced, as can a passport. Either is easier if you have a list of check numbers and your passport number kept separate from the originals. Make machine copies of your passport, travelers checks, credit cards, tickets, and itinerary. Leave one with a friend, carry one, and keep another in your suitcase. Carry only the credit cards you will be using. Have the issuing company telephone number in case they are lost or stolen.

Women should not carry valuables in their purses. In fact, it is better not to carry a purse. If you must carry significant sums of cash, men should place it in an inside pocket, and women should conceal it inside their clothing.

Wearing expensive jewelry or dressing conspicuously makes you a target. Thieves figure travelers carry money and other valuables. When casing crowds, they seek those they think will be most profitable as a mark.

If possible, pack only luggage you can carry yourself. It saves time and is easier to keep in sight. Mark luggage inside and out with name, address, and phone number. Outside luggage tags that hide your name and address are preferable.

Any carry-on luggage such as briefcases should be tagged and kept with you at all times. Any medications, business papers, and valuables that must be carried should be in luggage. A change of at least shirt, underwear, and socks comes in handy if other luggage is misplaced or is late in arriving.

Never let your carry-on luggage or purse out of your sight.

AIRLINES

Travel by air is a senior citizen favorite. The time saved in getting from one point to another, arriving reasonably fresh and ready to visit, sightsee, shop, or whatever is important. Air travel is also the safest form of travel. There are several things you can and should do to make certain you have a safe and secure journey.

As stated previously, obey airport security measures to the letter. When at the ticket counter, do not flash money and keep your eyes on your baggage. Watch closely when luggage is being tagged to your destination - make certain it is correctly tagged.

After dark in airports is "stay alert" time. Thieves like to prey on passengers between flights. If you have a companion, ask them to accompany you to restrooms, restaurants, and other spots. The criminal is a coward and likes to pick on loners. If traveling alone, and you do not feel safe, ask security to accompany you.

Be extra careful when you board your plane. If you have to climb a ladder, take it a step at a time and use the hand rails. Put your carry-on luggage where you can see it at a glance. Thieves ride airplanes just like you do.

If you require a special diet and was promised it when you booked your flight, notify the flight attendant. Air in planes is very dry, and if it has a negative effect on you, make it known.

In the event you are scheduled to catch a connecting flight and you are a late arrival - do not rush to make the connection. It is better to get re-booked and have your ticket validated by the airline that was responsible for the delay.

Any time you are out of the plane, keep your guard up. Try to stay in the vicinity of fellow passengers. Safety in numbers applies to anyone in a strange locale.

If a hijacker or terrorist situation arises, keep a low profile. Try to remain inconspicuous and do as you are ordered. Do not try to overpower these criminals by yourself and become a dead hero. If you are not the main target of a terrorist, you will probably weather the incident if you keep your head and do not panic.

When leaving the plane, take luggage you carried on and patiently move into the air terminal. Take note of any crowds and avoid getting caught in them.

Thieves target tourists believing they have money and other valuables. They use a number of ruses in their quest for loot. Included are these common ploys:

A. They bump into you to divert your attention and then grab for your wallet, purse or briefcase.

B. They will shout, trying to get your attention while a confederate picks your pocket.

C. They may spill a drink on you or your partner and use the diversion to steal from you.

D. An old favorite is to drop a roll of quarters near you and, then, steal your goods when you follow the natural tendency to retrieve the coins.

SHIPS

Precautions to take in boarding and debarking from a ship are the same as for the airlines. Security problems aboard a ship are magnified by the spirit of festivity that prevails. It is difficult to imagine a fellow passenger or crew member as a crook, but it happens.

The showing of large sums of cash, wearing expensive jewelry, or otherwise giving the impression you are loaded is asking for trouble.

As soon as you are on board and settled in your cabin, take a "security stroll". Learn the shortest path from your quarters to the deck and then time your return to your cabin. The time taken may not reflect your time in case of emergency because others may also be attempting to get "topside". Find more than one way to get from your sleeping area to the deck if possible. Locate lifeboats, life preservers, and fire extinguishers. If you can't find them, ask a member of the crew to help. After gathering this information, draw an outline of escape routes to take if trouble appears. Study any and all emergency procedures given you by the ship and commit them to memory.

The hour it takes to complete this task may be the best spent hour of your life. Then, if trouble comes, you are prepared. Those prepared and those who remain calm are usually those who survive.

Cruises are popular with Senior Citizens, and criminals are aware of the large number who enjoy them. The pickpocket and purse snatcher work crowds at departure and arrival piers. Con operators work on the ship during the cruise, and criminals at points of destination await your arrival.

If you are carrying large sums of money and taking expensive jewelry, have them put in the ship safety locker until needed.

The use of a portable alarm alerting you to

unwanted entry is worth considering. Check with the crew as to the use of other types of personal security items since there is always the possibility of mishaps at sea.

Senior Citizens like side tours and sightseeing trips cruise lines feature. If you go, stay alert. Tourists are strangers in a strange place and are considered easy marks. The roadside burglar or merchant may be using the activity to disguise criminal efforts. The pocket picking thief and purse snatcher may turn violent. Stay with your tour group, have a special "buddy" at all times, and if an incident arises, **STAY CALM!!** Always watch your wallet - always watch your purse.

TRAINS

Train travel has been increasing with improved Amtrak and other schedules. Senior Citizens - some on nostalgia trips - are high percentage users.

Facilities at most stations are not as comfortable and safe as they were at one time. Many depots and loading areas are in run- down neighborhoods. They leave much to be desired from many standpoints, particularly safety and security of the traveler. When purchasing tickets, ask about security measures available and how to get them. Railroads are responsible for the safety and welfare of their passengers.

After boarding a train, contact the conductor and discuss any security problems you might have.

Ask what action you should take in the event of a wreck, how to call for assistance in any kind of an emergency, and the expected response time.

After speaking with the conductor or other employee of the railroad, make your own security tour. Check exits at each end of the car you occupy. Walk to the dining car and lounge car. If there are observation decks and platforms, visit them, making mental notes of exits along the way.

As when using other types of public transportation, do not carry large sums of money and wear expensive jewelry. The train holdups of yesteryears are not common, but be prepared. The rules for watching wallets and holding tight to purses remain the same.

RV's AND CAMPERS

More recreation vehicles are on the road than ever - the majority of them driven by Senior Citizens. There are also huge numbers of self contained campers trailing behind autos and pickups - and again, the majority towed by Senior Citizens.

A relatively new industry has emerged from the ownership of these "homes on wheels", the facilities available campground. Even campgrounds in state and national parks offer some form of "campsites" with electrical outlets and hookups for sewerage disposal. And - as always, the addition of items to attract patrons also attracts the dregs of society.

RV and camper owners must be prepared for breakdowns on the road. The safety check list will indicate an ample supply of road flares, reflective signs, tow ropes, heavy duty jacks, and a tool kit. A CB radio, permanently mounted, or a portable model, easy to put into service when needed, is recommended. The citizens band is monitored by many road servicing organizations. CB operators furnish information such as local info, weather conditions, the condition of roads, and availability of campsites. The cost is small - potential returns high. Signs that an RV or trailer is equipped with a CB are deterrents to criminals; they wish to remain anonymous.

When checking into a campground, the first inquiry should be as to the quality and quantity of security available. Look over your assigned campsite before settling in. If it appears it might flood in the event of a heavy rain, is too close to vegetation presenting a fire hazard, or is on terrain that might cause tripping and falling - ask for another site.

As soon as you have completed settling in - take a stroll for security purposes. It is an excellent way to meet new people which is good security in itself. Check all possible exits and plan an escape route. Natural disasters such as floods, hurricanes, earthquakes, and tornados do not respect campers. Campers are more vulnerable to these exposures, but since you have your "home away from home" with you, prudent planning may allow you to escape damages.

Crime has not been a major problem in campgrounds except for the robbing of camp headquarters. But in a society as drug oriented as ours is becoming - especially with "crack" making each of us a potential source of enough cash to get a druggie high - it is becoming a problem.

AUTO TRAVEL

The Senior Citizens' favorite method of travel is by automobile. They use their own, they fly and rent, they sail and rent, and they rent to get around after train trips.

The security and safety suggestions in the chapter on automobiles apply when you travel in your car. In addition, several extra precautions should be taken.

If used in a foreign country (Canada and Mexico come to mind as they are frequently visited via private automobile) check with your insurance company and notify them of your trip so adequate coverage is afforded. Car rental agencies can provide you complete information regarding traffic laws, insurance requirements, and driving customs when you pick up your car. Take care of necessary items immediately.

Get off the road in a foreign country before dark. Whenever possible, travel with a companion or companions. Check with officials for recommended actions to take in the event of a breakdown. *Do Not Pick Up Hitchhikers, Anywhere or Anytime.* Avoid detours and do not stop in run down areas and in areas where questionable appearing people are congregated. If you run afoul of the law or have other problems, call the nearest American Embassy or Consulate. The State Department Bureau of Consular Affairs operates the citizens emergency center to aid Americans in trouble abroad. Get the telephone number of regular and emergency lines before you leave the U.S. and have it readily available.

CITIES

Seniors traveling to any city should obey safety rules and rules for security given in previous chapters. Cities worldwide are similar insofar as the human element is concerned.

Stay away from slum areas. Do not be conspicuous in any manner. Keep your wallet and purse protected, and do not flash money. Ask your lodging host questions pertaining to safety with emphasis on those areas you plan to visit any given time. If available, leave your valuables in the lodging safe and carry travelers' checks, small amounts of cash, and one or two credit cards.

Avoiding the use of drugs, heavy drinking, bars, and areas where unsavory characters gather is good security. Robbery and other major crimes against travelers, at home or abroad, often occur under circumstances that involve drug use or drinking in areas people would never think of entering in their home towns.

Travel in countries with language differences

makes the use of a guide a good investment. They can help you understand what you see and hear, and it is an excellent security measure.

RESORTS AND LODGING FACILITIES

Resort areas are favorites of Senior Citizens and the criminal - Seniors to enjoy themselves and criminals to work at their nefarious trade. Pickpockets, purse snatchers, and cat burglars join bunco artists, rapists, and thieves to prey on the relaxed and unsuspecting.

Many resorts now employ security personnel, some uniformed, some in plain clothes, to patrol grounds and watch over guests. In times past, visible security was considered to have a negative impact on guests, but the opposite is true today. Knowing management cares and is willing to take steps to protect is considered a plus.

Presence at a resort indicates rest, relaxation, and other forms of play. The chapter on recreation outlines some security measures advisable at resorts.

There are several items on the market Senior Citizens should investigate. They afford extra security for staying at resorts, motels, hotels, and bed and board facilities. Alarms set off by the turning of the door knob, jambs set inside doors to prevent easy entry, and portable sensors that detect movement are among the latest. You should notify security management when you use these protective items in the event of an emergency. No need to slow their efforts to rescue you.

It is always a good investment of your time to make a security check soon after you have settled in your quarters at any place away from home. Friends will not object if you ask what is required in the event of a natural disaster or fire while you are a guest in their home. Commercial institutions, including bed and board homes, should be happy you are interested in personal safety.

All possible exits and approximate time necessary to vacate the premises by the slowest member of your group should be noted along with the location of fire extinguishers and fire hoses. If door or window locks do not operate correctly, notify those responsible.

If you carry large sums of money or wear expensive jewelry, put them in a safe at commercial lodgings and determine where they may be safely stored when at a bed and board or private home.

LOBBIES, ELEVATORS, AND ROOM SERVICE

The criminal element has long favored hotel, motel, and resort lobbies as hangouts to spy on guests and listen to conversations at reservation and check in counters. You'll see them appearing as readers of newspapers or engaged in conversation with a confederate. They are ever alert to check ins and check outs. They learn room numbers, times of arrival, and other info they use to take advantage of the traveler.

A cardinal rule for everyone is the rule against entering an elevator with only one occupant alone. The robber and rapist knows how to stop the elevator between floors, and taking you by surprise is part of their operation that works far too often.

If you call for room service, have some personal code for each call. Using the old "room service" as means for entry works and is the easiest and most successful entry for the rapist and robber.

As in other phases of life, using common sense and taking safety and security measures will make travel more pleasurable.

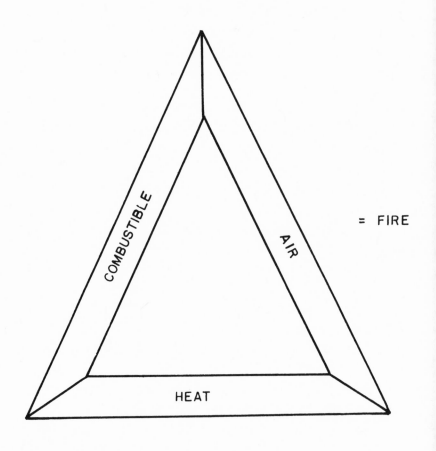

= FIRE

Chapter 9
FIRE

Other than infants and small children, Senior Citizens are most vulnerable to fire. Slower on foot and highly susceptible to smoke, more Senior Citizens lose their lives in fires than any other age group.

Firefighters, in the most dangerous of civilian occupations, have made great progress in controlling fires. Fires out of control, however, are still the most devastating of all disasters.

The advice given to yell "FIRE" when in any emergency situation is based upon the fact all humans fear fire. From the first time we burn ourselves to the day we die, we know what fire can do. (It doesn't ease our minds to hear about "fire and brimstone" being a future possibility!)

Fire, when controlled, is a great friend. It warms our bodies, cooks our food, furnishes light, and helps us remove remnants of plant and animal life. Uncontrolled, fire destroys forests, buildings, and almost anything else in its path. It pollutes water and air with ashes and toxic gases.

An unfriendly fire requires instant reaction. Although every fire is different, giving thought to what might happen, and how you would respond, is a must from a security standpoint. Fire safety means life safety.

RESIDENTIAL FIRE

Smoke detectors, fire extinguishers, and planning an escape route have been touched on in a previous chapter - now let's look closer.

SMOKE DETECTORS

The most dangerous fires are those that start at night while the family is asleep and those that start in another part of the house, trapping you away from an outside door.

The proper placement and maintenance of smoke and heat detectors helps overcome the dangers of fire by giving warnings. These devices respond loudly when temperatures rise or when smoke and bits of combustion are caused by the chemical and molecular changes during a fire.

Fire department personnel can help you plan the best location for these warning systems, or you may do it yourself. The general rules for selection and placement include:

1. Locate detectors between sleeping areas and most probable sources of fire. (Kitchen, furnace area, electrical fuse box area, and any area using space heaters - oil or electrically fueled).

2. Use either battery operated or electrically powered detectors but remember those

electrically powered do not work when outside power has been cut off. If you use them, test them at least once a month to be sure they respond. Battery powered detectors need testing weekly for battery strength. The grilles to each must be kept free of dust. Install only those devices that have been tested by a reliable organization such as Underwriters Lab.

3. Install the detectors on the ceiling or high on a wall a foot or less from the ceiling. Two or more detectors for the average house are recommended.

FIRE EXTINGUISHERS

There are a number of good fire extinguishers on the market. They are not expensive. You should have one in the kitchen, one in the garage, and one in the basement. The three classes of fire most homeowners might face are:

CLASS A - Known as a dry fire, it burns paper, wood, textiles.

CLASS B - Flammable liquid or grease burning.

CLASS C - Electrical fires.

CLASS D - Fire from chemicals or metals.

An extinguisher that will put out A, B, and C Class fires is called an ABC extinguisher. These extinguishers are charged with dry chemicals,

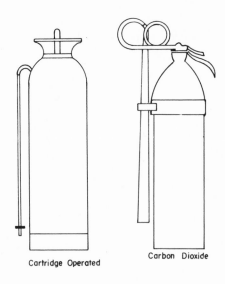

Cartridge Operated

Carbon Dioxide

nitrogen plus halon 1211, halon 1301, or ASP halonite. Choose one of them.

ESCAPE ROUTE

Establishing an escape route from the house and periodically using it in fire drills is a top priority security measure for Senior Citizens.

Sketching the layout of the house with escape routes is a project all occupants of the house should take part in. Each floor, including doors, windows, and stairways should be drawn as close to scale as possible. The location of those areas where fire is most likely to start should be marked in a color different than the rest of the sketch. The kitchen, where most house fires start should be the focal point.

If possible, two escape routes from each room should be worked out. Every obstruction along escape routes should be noted. If special escape windows or other exits require special efforts, they must be noted. (Many homes now have barred windows for burglary prevention, and they must be made easy to open from the inside for fire safety).

Designating a meeting place outside the house, timing the exit of the slowest member of the household, and assigning someone to assist those very young, very elderly, or physically impaired is a must.

FIRE SAFETY TIPS

A. Have fire department numbers at all telephone outlets.

B. Hold a fire drill using your escape route plan.

C. Do not smoke or allow anyone to smoke in bed.

D. Keep matches away from small children.

E. Do not store flammable liquids in the house or garage.

F. Use smoke detectors and keep fire extinguishers fully charged and handy.

G. Know how to safely use fuse boxes and circuit breaker panels.

H. Keep chimneys and flues soot free and in good repair.

I. Discard frayed electrical cords and do not use multiple attachment plugs.

J. Do not allow wide sleeve garmets around the stove.

K. Keep oily rags in tightly closed containers.

L. If and when fire breaks out - think - **DO NOT PANIC!**

MOBILE HOME FIRES

Inherent traits in the design, construction, and general placement of mobile homes has made them more susceptible to fire than other types of homes. The U.S. Department of Housing and Urban Development in a 1982 evaluation of mobile home fire safety said, "If you are a mobile home resident, you should know this about fire:

1. It occurs no more frequently in mobile homes than in structural residences.

2. It generally spreads faster in a mobile home.

3. Injuries occur more frequently from mobile home fires than others.

4. Mobile home occupants are twice as likely to die from a fire as occupants of other one or two-family residences."

The above paragraph is not intended to disparage mobile home living or the purchase of this type of shelter. The author, a former mobile home dweller, is following the goal of this book, to give

Senior Citizens the information necessary to ensure a safer and more secure life.

Most mobile home fires start in the kitchen. The living room fire, bedroom fire, heating room fire, and fires underneath the mobile home follow, in that order.

The prime causes of mobile home fires are found in the heating system and the electrical distribution system. Other fire causes, in order are: cooking, arson, appliances-a/c, and smoking.

Fire marshalls recommend mobile home dwellers take a close look at the following list of common fire hazards and correct any found.

1. The wall behind free standing stoves and fireplaces, not of fire resistant material.
2. Chimney not less than 3 feet above roof, without spark arrester, with trash on the roof, and with tree branches overhanging.
3. Aluminum wiring and overloaded electrical circuits.
4. Kitchen walls not of fire resistant material and without fire extinguisher.
5. Smoking in bed.
6. TV antenna poorly installed with loose guy wires and without lightning arresters.
7. Fuel tanks and water supply too close to house.
8. Skirting allowing under house storage and debris accumulation.

9. Lack of or poorly maintained smoke detectors.

10. Vegetation growing within 30 feet of house with burning barrel too close to house.

EMERGENCY ACTIONS

Mobile home dwellers should have a well planned escape route, practiced, without warning, several times each season.

When burning, mobile home materials emit toxic gases. Crawling on the floor where the air is fresher and cleaner is the safest way to exit.

Plan two escape routes from each room. When exiting a room through a door, feel the door before opening. If door is hot, do not open - fire is behind the door. Use another exit.

The time it takes the slowest occupant to get outside must be common knowledge.

Have a pre-arranged meeting place outside the home. When everyone is accounted for, permit no one to go back into the house.

MOBILE HOME FIRE PREVENTION TIPS

- Install and maintain smoke detectors

- Have the heating system overhauled annually

- Keep heater room free of any materials

- Have electrical system inspected annually - do not overload

- Be very cautious with space heaters if they must be used
- Debris and storage should not be allowed under the home
- Non-combustible walls should enclose heating system and kitchen areas
- Allow no one to smoke in bed
- Write an escape plan and practice it

UPPER FLOOR FIRES

Upper floor fires are most common in multi-story buildings such as apartments, condominiums, motels, and hotels. But - if you live in a two or more story house - general fire safety rules given here apply to you.

EXITS

Anytime you are a guest in a multi-story building, the first act after arriving at your room should be to check out the nearest exit. It may be the only chance you have to do so - and your life may depend upon it. Make it a habit - never deviate from it.

You - with companion or companions - should check the exit or exits. Discuss it and verbalize locations. Note aloud if exit is to the right or left of your room and if you must turn a corner to reach it. Open the exit door and look. Are there stairs or another door? If a door, open it and find the stairway. **Do not use elevators in a fire situation!** On the way back to your room, count the doors between your room and the exit door. In a smoke filled hallway, your life may depend on finding the right door.

Generally speaking, fire by-products such as smoke and gases are the real killers in fire situations - especially when combined with panic.

"Where there is smoke, there is fire" does not necessarily apply. The major cause of hotel fires (70%) is careless handling of smoking materials and matches. Smoldering mattresses produce great amounts of smoke. The smoke may be picked up by air handling equipment and drift into other areas. Once smoke is detected, leave the building.

When you check your route to the exit door, make a mental note of any obstacles in the hall. Ice machines, vending machines, and display cases are common.

IF SMOKE IS DETECTED

The key to your room should be placed in the same spot every time you stay in a hotel. The best location is on the night stand next to the bed.

Whenever you leave your room - and particularly during emergency situations - take your key with you. You should close your door when you leave, but conditions in the hall may force you to return - *Do not lock yourself out.*

The most important rule to follow in any fire situation is **DO NOT PANIC!** The worst enemy in

emergencies, panic is a state of being that is irreversible. When it sets in, people are rarely able to save themselves or assist others.

Smoke and gases rise, causing the eyes to burn and bringing on coughing. Getting on your hands and knees and crawling enables you to get the freshest air possible.

Feel any door before you open it - if it is hot - do not open. If you think you can make it to the exit, stay on the same side of the hallway counting doors until you reach the exit door. **Do not go to or get in an elevator!**

Entering the stairwell, start down, using the handrail. If you find smoke "stacked" on the way down, stop and start up. You should have a good grip on the handrail as you start up. Others may be coming down in a panic, and they may trample you if you don't hang on.

When you reach the roof, open the door and prop it open so smoke can vent itself from the stairwell. Go to the side of the roof from which the wind is blowing and wait until help arrives.

If you find the door of your room too hot to open, open the window to vent the smoke. Leave the window open unless outside smoke becomes too heavy. Keep your eye on it.

FIGHT FOR YOUR LIFE

If you are trapped by a fire, keep your head - *think* - **DON'T PANIC**. Help is on the way, and you must hold out until you are rescued. Some things you can do to save your life:

1. Use the telephone to let someone know where you are.
2. Open the bathroom vent and fill the tub.
3. Wet sheets or towels and stuff door cracks to keep out smoke.
4. Shut off fans and air conditioners.
5. Signal at your window with a flashlight.
6. If your door is hot, use the ice bucket and wet it down.
7. A mattress against the door wetted down may be needed.
8. If fire is outside the window, pull and wet down the drapes.

9. Wet a towel and tie around your nose for a filter.

10. If your clothes catch fire, drop to the floor and roll - if a blanket or sheet is handy - roll in it.

11. If burned - flush the burn with cold water for as long as you can.

12. **DO NOT GIVE UP!**

EMERGENCY EXITING

Fire authorities do not have a solid rule about jumping from burning buildings. It is generally felt jumps from the second floor, if you clear the building, may be done without fatal injury, but jumping from higher than the third floor usually results in death.

Most authorities agree that staying put, if you are trapped, and fighting for your life, without panic, is the best way to survive.

ARSON

The Department of Justice reports arson is among the fastest growing crimes. The arsonist burns buildings, automobiles, and trash cans. Arson becomes a concern of Senior Citizens because it affects the entire community in which they live.

Most arson fires are set by vandals or revenge seekers. The vandals are usually teenagers who like the excitement of a fire and like the idea of destroying property. Arson for revenge fires fit no set group, but argumentive lovers, fired employees, and participants in violent quarrels are often guilty.

The impact of arson reaches all segments of society and is exceptionally hard on Senior Citizens. Arson turns neighborhoods into areas of decay and falling property prices.

Seniors often do not have the chance to move and recoup. Seniors lose their lives more often than others in any kind of fire. Arson results in abandoned building attracting more vandals who like to prey on Seniors. The tax base in burned neighborhoods falls and taxes increase on those who remain.

Senior Citizens can help protect their property by:

1. Storing flammable liquids and materials used to start fires.

2. Cleaning up rubbish piles and disposing of materials used in arson fires.

3. Keeping property well lighted at night.

4. Keeping smoke alarms in good repair in their homes and businesses.

5. Informing authorities of suspicious fires.

6. Organizing an arson prevention and detection program in the neighborhood.

7. Talking to your local fire department about arson prevention tactics.

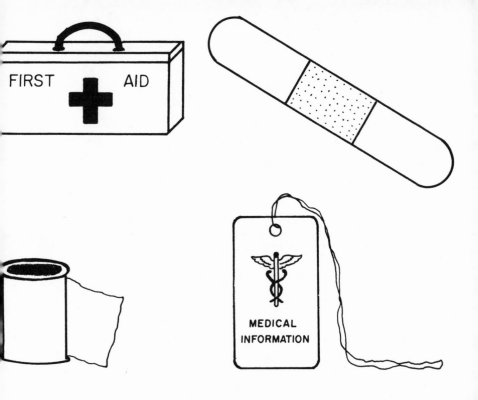

Chapter 10
FIRST AID

This chapter is not intended to give professional medical advice or substitute for proper first aid training. It is for reference and to remind Senior Citizens that knowing basic first aid procedures may save their lives or the life of another. It is also to remind Senior Citizens that being secure requires staying healthy.

The American Red Cross conducts many courses in first aid, CPR, and related subjects. They welcome Seniors. If you would like to lend a hand and get some real self satisfaction, give them a call.

Your personal physician is the best source of information on health problems and will advise correct habits to follow.

FIRST AID KITS

A number of companies make first aid kits for individuals and also furnish refills. You find them in pharmacies, drug stores, and other retail outlets.

Senior Citizens at work need to know the location and contents of workplace first aid supplies. The office first aid kit should be in a readily accessible area and replenished as necessary. First aid kits in other work areas should be larger and contain a greater number of items. If companies employ medical personnel, they should be responsible for first aid and emergency supplies.

The home first aid kit should contain ample supplies for the number of occupants. Home kits should be kept in areas other than the bathroom. The high humidity in bathrooms may reduce effectiveness of the contents.

The Food and Drug Administration of the Department of Health and Human Services has suggested a list of items for home medical needs. The list includes non-drug and drug items. It states the selection of health care items for the family medicine chest is a matter of common sense and that each family may have specific needs. This is the list.

Non-Drug Products
Assorted sizes of adhesive bandages
Gauze - in pads and in a roll
Absorbent cotton
Adhesive tape
Elastic bandage
Small blunt-end scissors
Tweezers
Fever thermometer Hot water bottle
Heating pad
Eye cup for flushing eyes
Ice bag
Correct dosage spoon
Vaporizer or humidifier
And - very important - a first aid manual

Drug Items
Analgesic - aspirin or its substitute for your situation
Emetic - syrup of ipecac to induce vomiting and activated charcoal
Antacid
Antiseptic solution
Hydrocortisone cream for skin problems
Calamine lotion for poison ivy and skin irritations
Petroleum jelly

Drug Items (continued)
    Anti-diarrhetic
    Non-supressant type cough syrup
    Decongestant
    Burn ointment
    Anti-bacterial topical ointment

In addition to these items, you may want to have a laxative, anti-nausea medicine, rubbing alcohol, hydrogen peroxide, linament, an insect repellant, and a 15 (or above) rated sunscreen solution.

If your grandchildren or other small children visit your home, you need to keep your medicines and first aid supplies out of their reach. Seniors often ask for regular caps for their medications since child-resistant caps are difficult to remove. They must never fall into tiny hands. Keep medicines on a high shelf in a bedroom closet or hall - perhaps in a box that can be locked. If you lock them up, be sure the key is easily found.

Keep prescription and non-prescription drugs in separate containers. A list attached to containers makes it easier to find items.

Some drugs need refrigeration. Keep them in a special place, away from food items, and label them.

Check medicines frequently for amounts, freshness, and expiration dates. When disposing of outdated or no longer needed drugs, flush them down the toilet.

An emergency phone list should be taped inside the medicine storage container, in the bathroom cabinet, and near every phone in the house. The list should have fire, police, poison control, rescue squad, hospital, and physician numbers in large legible numbers.

Every vehicle should have a first aid kit. The kit should be kept in the passenger area. Trunk lids may be hard to open after an accident. The kit will give you peace of mind and may prove to be a lifesaver for you or others on the road. Many RV owners take the home medicine and first aid kits with them on extended trips, keeping them up-to-date and filled.

EMERGENCY SITUATIONS

There are five basic life or death situations to recognize and act upon. They are serious, demanding immediate medical attention, but your knowledge of them plus quick thinking and actions might save a life.

1. Stoppage of breathing. If the average person stops breathing, it must be restored in 3 to 6 minutes or the person may die. Irreversible brain damage can occur in 4 minutes. Whatever causes the breathing to stop, electrical shock, drowning, choking, overdosing on drugs, or swallowing the tongue, first aid must be swift. Actions to take include using the "Heimlich Maneuver" to dislodge food from the throat, getting the head of the victim back and jaw forward, checking the mouth and throat for food, gum, dirt, or other matter, and pulling the tongue out if swallowed. If breathing doesn't start at once, begin mouth-to-mouth artificial respiration.

2. Stoppage of the heart. If victim is conscious, help give any prescribed medication (if known). Have the victim lie down and get to a hospital as rapidly as possible. The treatment to restore flow of blood from the heart is known as CPR - cardiopulmonary resuscitation - and should be attempted only by properly trained persons. Improperly executed, the technique might cause the victim great harm.

3. Bleeding and hemorrhage. A person can bleed to death in less than two minutes! The average adult body has six quarts of blood and the loss of one quart may be fatal. The quickest way to stop external bleeding is by placing pressure directly on the wound. It is fast, direct, and often the best method.

The three types of external bleeding, with emergency first aid control measures are:

Venous Bleeding: Coming from a vein, the blood is usually dark red flowing in a steady stream. Apply direct pressure to the wound with compress bandage or handkerchief. A bare hand pressed against the wound may allow time fore the blood to clot - usually three to six minutes.

Capillary Bleeding: Blood oozes from the capillaries into the wound. Direct pressure with compress bandage, handkerchief, or the bare hand ordinarily stops the bleeding since capillary blood clots rapidly.

Arterial Bleeding: Blood comes from an artery, bright red and in gushes or spurts. This is the most serious type of bleeding and must be stopped very quickly. The heart is pumping blood into the artery and blood loss is rapid. Place a compress bandage, handkerchief, or hand directly on the wound and keep pressure on until help arrives.

> *Use of a tourniquet is not recommended. If it must be used (to stem the bleeding of a severed limb), tell the first medical person **how long** it has been in place.*

Internal Bleeding: Internal bleeding cannot be treated by an untrained person. If such bleeding is suspected, keep victim quiet and treat for shock.

4. Poisoning: There are three classes of poisoning and ***the first step in the treatment of any poison is to call the poison center and a doctor.***

External Poisoning. Poisons on the skin or eyes from chemicals, gases, acids, or burning metal. Eyes should be bathed with warm water from a container for at least 15 minutes and until poison center or doctor assistance is available. If on the skin, remove clothing from affected parts, flood the skin with water, wash with soap and water, then rinse repeatedly.

Internal (swallowed) Poison. Any number of swallowed items may be poisonous and may cause serious illness or death.

Medicines: Overdoses or mistaken doses of medicine are common. They should not be treated by mouth without specific medical knowledge. Call the poison center and a doctor immediately.

Chemicals: Household products are the most common sources of poisoning. If victim is conscious and can swallow, give milk or water to dilute. Call poison center and doctor to learn if you should make victim vomit. (Lye, bleaches, and ammonia cause burning when vomiting).

Other Items: Plant materials, garage and garden products and personal products are often swallowed, accidentally or on purpose. Other than for milk or water for dilution purposes, wait for instructions from poison center, doctor, or pharmacist.

174

Internal (inhaled) Poisoning. Immediately move victim into fresh air. Give mouth-to-mouth resuscitation if necessary and call the poison center and doctor. There are many sources of internal (inhaled) poisoning. Most of them are connected with some sort of burning process. There are forest fires, chemical fires, residential fires, and commercial property fires. Other sources include carbon monoxide from automobile and other engines and inversion pollution in hot weather. Our lungs are more sensitive than we have suspected (witness lung cancer from smoking and devastation from emphysema).

Other Poisons: There are many other forms of poisoning. Poison ivy, poison oak, and poison sumac attack bare skin as do numbers of other plants. Individuals may have allergies resulting in painful reactions when certain materials are used or contacted. Personal products in the perfume, deodorant, and shampoo lines plus paints, flammable liquids, insecticides, and fertilizers may be culprits. Cleansing the skin after contact and refusing to use known contaminants is about all that can be done to help in such situations.

5. Shock. The fifth life or death situation - and one almost always present when a serious illness or injury occurs - is a physiological reaction to some form of bodily trauma resulting in loss of blood pressure and slowing of vital life processes. Shock is a killer! Learn the symptoms and treat it quickly.

The symptoms of shock include, but are not limited to, the following:

A. Rapid but weak pulse.

B. Skin cool to the touch - forehead clammy.

C. Lips and fingernails pale - turning blue.

D. Victim is chilling.

E. Victim is nauseated.

F. Pupils dilate.

G. Victim is thirsty.

First aid for shock includes:

1. Keeping victim lying down with feet elevated unless there is apparent head or chest injury.

2. Loosen clothing but keep victim warm. Do not apply heat but maintain body heat present.

3. Treat injuries but do not let victim see injuries.

4. Reassure victim - tell that help is coming - all will be well.

5. Remember - keep body temperature from falling - shock is a killer.

OTHER EMERGENCY
FIRST AID SITUATIONS

In Any Emergency Situation: Treat for shock and keep victim as comfortable as possible.

Unconsciousness: The victim is unconscious. The face is red. The eyes are fixed and there are symptoms of paralysis. Breathing is irregular or perhaps stopped. The unconsciousness may have been caused by stroke, heart attack, diabetic coma, electrical shock, concussion, extreme heat, or cold. If the reason is unknown - loosen the clothing, keep the body warm and treat for shock.

Fractures: If victim has a fracture or is suspected to have one, do not move if it can be avoided. Keep the victim warm and dry. Treat for shock. If fracture is compound and bleeds - control bleeding. Make temporary splint from sticks, newspapers, or other light materials. Place splint around break extending past the joint above and the joint below the fracture.

Burns: Chemical burns should be flushed with as much fresh water as is possible. The cleaner the area becomes the better are chances for recovery. Scalding burns from water or steam and burns from open flames or contact with heated objects tend to send victims into shock. *Do not apply salves, creams, or ointments to burns.*

IN ANY FIRST AID SITUATION

There are a number of things that should not be attempted when giving first aid. First aid is emergency help until medically trained personnel arrive, or the victim arrives at a medical post.

Here are ten **"Do Nots"**:

1. Do not give any form of medicine.
2. Do not try to remove an object or objects from the eye.
3. Do not give liquids to unconscious persons.
4. Do not lift injured persons to sitting or standing positions.
5. Do not move persons with fractures or if internal injuries are suspected.
6. Do not put ointments, creams, or salves on burns.
7. Do not restrain epilectic seizures.
8. Do not allow victims to see their injuries.
9. Do not discuss injuries with unauthorized persons.
10. Do not give a victim up for dead until medical personnel so advise.

Closing this section on first aid, the author suggests you look into the "good samaritan" laws in the state in which you reside. Many suits have been instigated against individuals who attempted to help a stricken person.

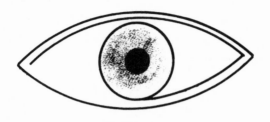

NEIGHBORHOOD WATCH

Chapter 11
ET CETERA

The "it only happens to someone else" syndrome is common among Senior Citizens. Having lived to become Seniors, we get the feeling we are somehow immune to further assaults and will be allowed to live the remainder of our lives peacefully and secure.

Realistically, nothing is further from fact. We are subject to all criminal acts and are exposed to every other ill that can befall a human being. The only thing we can boast of is that we have lived a long time without succumbing and that we have managed to survive the onslaughts.

We live in an America ever undergoing change. Some of it good, some of it bad. We have modern plumbing and electrical power. We glory in the medical advances that eliminated polio, scarlet fever, and typhoid and yellow fever.

Tooth decay is becoming passe as dentists provide almost painless repairs and preventative care. We are able to get a new heart, new eyes, a new liver, and severed limbs reattached. We send citizens to the moon, produce enough food to feed the world and are hailed as the most peace loving superpower on earth.

On the down side, we have the highest criminal rate of any industrialized nation. Muggings, rapes, robberies, burglaries, drug use, arson, and murder make daily headlines. With overcrowded jails and prisons, felons are back on the street before security personnel and law enforcement personnel have completed and filed arrest reports. Death rows bulge as lenient courts and judges protect the criminal while victims are forgotten. With an estimated 90% of the world's lawyers, we have become the most litigous nation on earth. Lawsuits clog the court system while the criminal element enjoys the "revolving door", in today, out tomorrow.

Having survived youth and middle age durings periods less prone to violence and treachery, Senior Citizens must keep abreast of every method

Etc.

available to ensure security and peace of mind during their golden years.

AIDS

During the past decade, Acquired Immunity Disorder Syndrome (AIDS) has appeared, creating havoc and endangering our entire population. An incurable disease, attacking homosexuals and intravenous drug users for the most part, it has spilled over into normal society. Using contaminated blood supplies in transfusions and having sexual relations with infected partners appear to be the main sources of infection of heterosexuals. Much remains to be learned about the disease and how it is transmitted.

Senior Citizens as a group have been least affected by this scourge. Perhaps their primarily monogamous lifestyle and lack of exposure is responsible. However - Senior Citizens undergo many operations requiring transfusions. If you are going to need a blood transfusion - discuss it with your physician and surgeon.

RAPE

Professionals tell us rape is not a crime of passion but one of violence. Whatever your opinion, facts show the rapist does not exempt any age female from being a victim. Youngsters of either sex are attacked by these deviates. Senior Citizens, having less physical strength, are very susceptible.

The best defense against rape is to avoid

situations where the crime can be committed. And, keep in mind, it can happen to anyone. Have a companion with you when out at night, when you go to a public restroom, or when you must visit sparsely populated localities. Do not pick up strangers anywhere. Never enter an elevator with a lone male and do not make it appear you are "available". Don't take chances on "lonely heart" or "dating" clubs.

Do not let unidentified persons into your home. If you work in the yard, keep an eye peeled for strangers and be prepared to get in the house and lock the door.

Authorities report most rapes are committed by someone who knows the victim even though the acquaintance may have been a short one.

If you are attacked, yell "FIRE" as loud as you can - for as long as you can. If possible, try to talk yourself out of the situation by appealing for a sense justice. Remind him his mother and sister may someday be a victim. Other defense actions to take depend upon you as an individual. In any event - be able to identify him later!!!

Rape prevention classes are taught by almost every law enforcement group in the U.S. Contact your local force and sign up. If you have been a victim - contact your local rape crisis network - they provide support, and you can offer support to other victims.

If you are raped - report it as quickly as possible. Get to a health facility before attempting

Etc.

to clean up. There is no shame in being raped - and reporting it may save another. It is imperative for your own health. Rapists get AIDS and other venereal diseases and may make you a double victim.

CON ARTISTS

Senior Citizens are a favorite target of all types of con men and women. These "artists", as they are known to bunco squad and fraud investigators, figure the senior citizen has resources. They know the senior with reduced or absent earning power would like to increase income from presently held savings or investments. They hope the years have taken away some mental sharpness making for easier victims.

Unfortunately, this profile fits many Seniors. Anxious to add to resources and motivated by greed, many Seniors fall into the hands of unscrupulous operators.

You've heard it many times and will hear it again and again. The difficulty is to remember it. Here it is - in capital letters and underlined:

IF IT SOUNDS TOO GOOD TO BE TRUE
IT PROBABLY IS.

Scams against Senior Citizens are numerous. Some scams, with suggested ways to protect yourself against them include:

Official Looking Envelopes. If it doesn't have the government stamp on it - it didn't come from a government agency. If it so implies, show it to postal authorities and ignore the contents.

Unsolicited Telephone Calls: Tell 'em you aren't interested at the beginning. (The author has an aunt who listens to the entire spiel then sweetly says, "What did you say?") If these callers persist, report them to the telephone company, the Better Business Bureau, and the law. Do not give them your social security number, let them know how many people live in the house, or any other information. They may be casing your home for future criminal actions.

Door To Door Offers: It is better to tell them you are not interested or do not have time to talk. If you had an interest in a product and asked for a salesperson, after properly identifying them, take your time, understand it thoroughly, get any and all agreements in writing, in simple terms, and insist on a provision for getting your money back in full. Honest salespeople happily agree to this.

Unsolicited Merchandise: If you receive something you did not order, you do not have to pay for it. You can return the unopened package marked "Return To Sender" - no charge to you. You can open the package and keep whatever was sent or throw it away. (Sending C.O.D. packages and items supposedly ordered by a deceased person is a scam practiced by some who study obituary columns and immediately send merchandise. Do not accept them.)

Bait And Switch: The ad says valuable items

are on sale at fabulous discounts. When you get to the store, it is slightly damaged, and you are urged to purchase a more expensive model. Insist on buying the item advertised or refuse to buy anything and report the merchant to the Better Business Bureau.

Mail Fraud: You may receive mail saying you have won something. If you were not a contest participant - throw it away. The merchandise you "won" is usually part of an item. You must buy added parts to make it useful. The cost of the addition will be more than the whole is worth. Or - you may have been "discovered" to be an heir to oilfield or gold mine fortunes. If you send some money, you will receive full details. Any time you suspect mail fraud, ask your postal authorities to put you in touch with a postal inspector.

Medical And Health Fraud: Use only medical facilities and products recommended by your doctor or health clinic. "Miracle drugs" and "Miracle cures" are for the benefit of those who advertise them. Reputable physicians and pharmaceutical companies do not guarantee anything other than the best effort possible and purity of products.

Repair Fraud: Do not use the door to door "happen to be in the area" repair person. If you need repairs to home, appliances, or vehicles, get several detailed written estimates. Watch that you don't get stuck paying for the estimate. Get a guarantee for work completed and test the repair work before you pay.

Professional Consultation: Before consulting a professional architect, physician, engineer, landscaper, or CPA, ask about fees. If you go to a lawyer, have, in writing, a detailed list of all costs including initial visit spelled out. Never allow them to make any move until after fees have been discussed, written down, and agreed upon.

Charity Fraud: Make any and all charity donations by check and send by mail with their address on check. Make sure the charity is legitimate and one you think has a good purpose.

Self Improvement Scams: T h o r o u g h l y investigate any diet plan, dance club, personality clinic, sleep learning, or language improvement pitches and ask to talk to a number of users and former participants. Few of us become expert dancers, linguists, lose weight, or become charmers without great amounts of work.

Land Fraud: Never buy land without seeing it. Always ask for the HUD report before buying from a land developer. Call the U.S. Soil Conservation Service for a land analysis. Real estate may be a good investment, but it has limited liquidity qualities and Senior Citizens may not have the time to see increases in value.

Business Opportunities: Be wary of work-at-home ventures, franchises, vending machine operations, and other "invest in, then work" schemes. Check any business opportunity with Better Business Bureaus and Chambers of

Commerce. Make certain all "opportunities" are in writing with guarantees.

Investment Frauds: Senior Citizens are solicited for all types of "get rich quick" investment deals. The "pyramid franchise", where a dealership is purchased, and you get others to work for you, is most common. "You get 10 distributors, then they get 10, and then each of them get 10" is the pitch. Figure it out - who will be left to buy? If you are asked to set up a dealership - ask who buys left over product. Investment companies offering above normal returns on investments should be suspect as should stock offers that are the "chance of a lifetime".

Con Games: There are many tricks used to con Seniors and others out of money and other possessions. "Cons" - male and female - are generally friendly people with "honest" faces, whatever they are. They are alert and creative and appear in many guises. They work on people who do not know them. If a stranger offers you something for nothing or a ridiculously low price - watch out! If anyone asks you to make a bank withdrawal for *any reason* - refuse and report. If you are asked about your financial worth or you are asked to pay large sums in cash - be alert. Two of the most used scams (and being used as you read this) are the following:

The Pigeon Drop: You are approached by someone who has "found" a large sum of cash wanting to know if you "lost" it. When you say no, the "finder" wishes to share it with you as a gesture of friendliness, but you must first put up some type of cash "good faith" collateral. When you put up your money, the "find", the "finder", and your cash disappear.

The Bank Examiner. You are approached by someone posing as a bank examiner who wishes your help in catching a dishonest bank employee. You are to withdraw cash and give to the "examiner" to check the serial numbers. When you turn over the cash, you never see it or the "examiner" again.

If you are ever conned or defrauded - report the incident. The knowledge you may help save someone else and may have the criminal imprisoned should make up for any embarassment suffered.

FIREARMS

Senior Citizens have joined other Americans in a wave of weapon buying. They fear the criminal element and realize law enforcement has been severely limited by lenient laws, lenient courts, and low budgets. They arm themselves to help in the fight. The right to own firearms is constitutional and as long as you obey state laws regarding their possession and use, you may have your choice. However - it is suggested you buy only quality firearms, know how to use them properly, and take courses or refresher courses on an approved range from a competent instructor. Using a firearm safely requires practice as does any other activity.

Etc.

PARTICIPATING IN CRIME PREVENTION

Senior Citizens may be the best defense against crime. They have the time, the experience, and the ability to gain the knowlege needed in combatting criminals and criminal activities.

Numbers of local, state, and national programs desparately need volunteers for programs already in action. The McGruff-"Take a bite out of crime" program and the neighborhood watch program are examples.

The neighborhood child safety designation decal needs to be seen in more windows.

Reporting crimes and suspicious appearing individuals helps reduce crime in many areas.

Having law enforcement and security personnel as guests at PTA, civic, and fraternal meetings makes them feel better about their jobs. It allows you to get to know them and how you can be of assistance as they labor to protect you.

Cooperating with your local fire department, getting to know their personnel, and having fire drills on schedule is good for their morale and may help save your life and property.

To go into every security and safety measure and to point out every danger would take far more space than allowed herein. But, if you follow any of the recommendations for your security and safety that you read in this book that you haven't been following, you will be a more secure senior citizen and your golden years will be safer years.

NOTES

INDEX

Index

ABOUT THE AUTHOR

DAVID Y. COVERSTON, author of *Security For Senior Citizens*, won the National Association of Independent Publishers 1986 Best Book Content award for his book, *Security Guard*. Past President of Florida Security Guard and Private Investigators with memberships in American Association Industrial Security and Florida Peace Officers Association, he served on the subcommittee for security officer education, Private Security Advisory Council for the Florida Department of State. Editor of Security Personnel Newsletter for National Association Security Personnel, the native Oklahoman resides in Ocala, Florida.

SECURITY SEMINARS PRESS
Post Office Box 70162
Ocala, Florida 32670
Security Seminars Press publishes books, manuals, newsletters, and other educational materials relating to security. Security Personnel Newsletter is a bi-monthly publication of the National Association Security Personnel whose membership is open to anyone interested in personal or professional security. For information, write us!